"*An Impossible Marriage* is a boo[ ] sible but for any marriage, especially between Christians. Through their own story, Matt and Laurie graciously put before the reader the purpose of marriage—the great mystery and seeming impossibility of Christ being made one with his church."

Matt Chandler, author, pastor, and president of Acts 29 Network;
and **Lauren Chandler,** author, speaker, and singer/songwriter

"Sometimes, what seems impossible becomes surprisingly possible—if someone just shows you how to turn and see everything from a completely different perspective. Let Laurie and Matt Krieg be your trusted guides, turn these unforgettable pages—and find yourself turning to see everything in a fresh way—turning to see the face of God. Who, right before your eyes, can make the impossible into a glorious possible."

Ann Voskamp, author of *The Broken Way* and *One Thousand Gifts*

"A courageous, bold, and vulnerable story showing the lengths God will go to for us to experience true love and intimacy."

Gabe Lyons, president of Q Ideas and author of *Good Faith*

"Every time I hang out with Laurie and Matt, I see Jesus on the throne of their marriage. Not because they have that gooey, mushy, always-in-love-and-never-a-fight marriage. They don't. (And who does?) Instead, their marriage radiates meaning, depth, authenticity, genuine joy, and a cross-shaped shadow that points to the real meaning of marriage—Christ's unyielding love for his people. Laurie and Matt's marriage shows off the gospel in all its truth and grace, which is why I'm so excited they decided to write this book. Anyone who is married or considering getting married *needs* to read *An Impossible Marriage.*"

Preston Sprinkle, the Center for Faith, Sexuality, and Gender

"With *An Impossible Marriage*, Laurie and Matt Krieg have offered us a living, redemptive sacrifice—a story of durable hard work and of beauty, goodness, and joy that emerges out of trauma and shame and grief, as all the best stories do. In a world of diminished, atrophied imagination, our authors invite us to risk our hearts, reimagining not merely marriage but all of life as it can be in this present age and as it will be in the age to come. Read this book, practice what you read, and become the love of our triune God."

Curt Thompson, author of *The Soul of Shame* and *Anatomy of the Soul*

"*An Impossible Marriage* reminded me of my longing to hear from Jesus in every aspect of my life, not only my marriage. Honestly written with a bent toward those who have battled trauma, this unique marriage book will inspire you to surrender your life and your marriage to Jesus afresh."

Mary DeMuth, author of *We Too: How the Church Can Respond Redemptively to the Sexual Abuse Crisis*

"I love Matt and Laurie's journey. But more than loving their journey, I love Matt and Laurie. Period. *An Impossible Marriage* is an inestimable gift to the body of Jesus in this season. It is theologically poignant, emotionally authentic, intellectually honest, spiritually freeing, and mission-ally critical. It has gospel bite and rawness. It's sassy and tender and strong and bold. Their adventurous journey slows down just enough to invite us all in, and it speeds up just enough to keep us all from becoming emotionally and spiritually complacent. On their walk to Emmaus, the risen Christ meets and walks with them in the darkness of their despondency and confusion, listens to their dashed hopes and overflowing frustrations, and gently nudges them—and I dare say us—toward gospel hope and redemptive joy. They yield again and again. Their journey is a seesaw of lament and joy, Good Friday and Resurrection Sunday. The living God is giving Matt and Laurie what to desire—him. I realized midway through that *An Impossible Marriage* is as much about my own yielding to Christ and my own oneness with God and my wife as it is about Matt and Laurie's. Like Matt and Laurie, may we all surrender to God and want what he wants."
Marvin Williams, lead pastor of Trinity Church in Lansing, Michigan, devotional writer, *Our Daily Bread*

"As a celibate gay Christian and former anti-Christian gay activist, I once thought a marriage like Matt and Laurie's was a sheer impossibility. I now deeply admire this book, just as I do its authors. There is no distance between who I know them to be and what is written in these pages. Matt and Laurie's tenacious example and heart-wrenching journey of finding God's redemptive plan for marriage is a must-read not just for every Christian but especially for those who are entirely perplexed by the notion of a marriage like theirs. This book's brave authenticity reveals how marriage in and through Jesus as Lord becomes a glorious sign of hope not despite but through our beautiful and broken humanity. Matt and Laurie's refreshing resolve and conviction for biblical truth alongside their heartfelt identification with the LGBTQI+ community is a rare jewel that takes us beyond the worn debate that the question of sexuality invokes. *An Impossible Marriage* is not just a one-of-a-kind book on marriage; it's also a prophetic message that frees us from the idol of sex and marriage in and outside the church that has too long kept us bound from knowing the transformative power and ineffable goodness of the love and holiness of God."
David Bennett, speaker and author of *A War of Loves*

"In these raw and daring pages, we come face to face with the love of Jesus— a love that aches and bleeds and never lets go. This book is the story of a marriage, yes, but it's also the story of The Marriage between a divine Lover and the bride for whom he died. Whether you're single or married, straight or gay or anything else, there's something of the gospel for you here."
Gregory Coles, author of *Single, Gay, Christian*

LAURIE KRIEG *and* MATT KRIEG

AN IMPOSSIBLE
MARRIAGE

WHAT OUR MIXED-ORIENTATION
MARRIAGE HAS TAUGHT US ABOUT
LOVE AND THE GOSPEL

An imprint of InterVarsity Press
Downers Grove, Illinois

InterVarsity Press
P.O. Box 1400, Downers Grove, IL 60515-1426
ivpress.com
email@ivpress.com

Published in association with the literary agency of Wolgemuth & Associates.

InterVarsity Press® is the book-publishing division of InterVarsity Christian Fellowship/USA®, a movement of students and faculty active on campus at hundreds of universities, colleges, and schools of nursing in the United States of America, and a member movement of the International Fellowship of Evangelical Students. For information about local and regional activities, visit intervarsity.org.

Unless otherwise indicated, all Scripture quotations are taken from the Holy Bible, New Living Translation, copyright ©1996, 2004, 2007, 2013. Used by permission of Tyndale House Publishers, Inc., Carol Stream, Illinois 60188. All rights reserved.

While any stories in this book are true, some names and identifying information may have been changed to protect the privacy of individuals.

Cover design and image composite: David Fassett
Interior design: Daniel van Loon
Images: blue abstract watercolor: © kostins / iStock / Getty Images Plus
　　　　flame painting: © Pobytov / DigitalVision Vectors / Getty Images
　　　　abstract watercolor: © lutavia / iStock / Getty Images Plus
　　　　postage stamp edge border: © troyek / E+ / Getty Images
　　　　black abstract watercolor: © gedzun / iStock / Getty Images Plus
　　　　abstract snowfall: © Pobytov / DigitalVisions Vectors / Getty Images
　　　　watercolor abstract: © Sergey Ryumin / Moment Collection / Getty Images
　　　　abstract watercolor: © mikroman6 / Moment Collection / Getty Images

ISBN 978-0-8308-4793-8 (print)
ISBN 978-0-8308-4794-5 (digital)

Printed in the United States of America ♾

Library of Congress Cataloging-in-Publication Data
A catalog record for this book is available from the Library of Congress.

P	25	24	23	22	21	20	19	18	17	16	15	14	13	12	11	10	9	8	7	6	5	4	3	2	1
Y	36	35	34	33	32	31	30	29	28	27	26	25	24	23	22	21	20								

This book is for Gwyn, Juliette, and Ellis. We pray that anything Christlike the world reads in these pages matches the reality of your experience in our home.

CONTENTS

PROLOGUE

IT IS IMPOSSIBLE

Humanly speaking, it is impossible.
But with God everything is possible.

MATTHEW 19:26

LAURIE

People say our marriage is impossible. They're right.

My husband, Matt, and I are in what some call a "mixed-orientation marriage," meaning that, for at least one of us, our default sexual attraction is not toward the gender of our spouse. It's toward our same gender. In our marriage, that would be me: my default attraction is not toward men but women. Matt's is toward women too.

When we speak about our marriage publicly, or one-on-one with new friends, they often respond to our marriage description by cocking their heads like a puppy learning a new command. "I'm sorry, what? I don't get it." Depending on how comfortable they feel, they might even articulate their confusion. "So, are you attracted to your husband at all? How does that work?"

The implication is, "Your marriage is impossible."

It is impossible . . . if we don't understand what marriage is for.

Underneath the question, "How does that work?" are unspoken questions that expose what we believe about marriage. "How in the world do you have a sexual relationship with your spouse if you aren't naturally attracted to him? Isn't the purpose of marriage—or at least the glue that holds it together—sex? And to have sex in a marriage, don't you need attraction?"

In this understanding, the goal of marriage seems to be the kind of unity that results in the climax of many chick flicks: the couple sleeps together.

It is fascinating to us because no one ever publicly asks Matt if he wrestles with attraction toward me. No one seems to even *think* to ask it. The implied statement behind the lack of questions for him reveals something of the audience's beliefs about marriage and men: *Matt is a man. He must always be ready to have sex with his wife. Sex fuses marriages together. Therefore, perhaps, he is the one holding the marriage together.*

Little do they realize, Matt's attraction toward women almost imploded our marriage. For five years, Matt hid a pornography addiction that began not because of sexual issues as a result of my orientation but because he bowed to the same idol many do—thinking that sex would bring him the fulfillment he craved.

But it didn't. It doesn't. It can't.

Just because Matt is attracted to women doesn't mean our marriage is whole.

Just because I am attracted to women doesn't mean our marriage is broken.

As we speak more openly about our marriage, straight women open up about their marriage struggles too: "When I share my lack of desire to have sex with my husband, other women tell me, 'Just do it, and then he will open up emotionally to you.' Or, 'Pray that God will put passion into your marriage.' Or, 'Feel sexy so that you want to have sex.' I mostly feel guilty because my mind wanders during sex, and I am hardly attracted to him at all."

We hear the exchange rate for emotional connection. *Sex will satisfy him (and get him off my back), and I'll get what I want.* We hear the idolatry. *Emotional connection will scratch the itch of my heart.* We hear the lack of *natural* attraction.

Straight men open up about their marriage struggles when we speak too: "I love my wife, but I can't stop looking at pornography." Or, "After thirty years, I wrestle with desiring her at all." Or, "I hear sex begins in the kitchen. I serve her and meet her emotional needs, and then I get what I want."

Again, we hear the exchange rate for connection. *Emotional connection will satisfy her (and get her off my back), and I'll get what I want.* We hear the idolatry. *Sex will scratch the itch of my heart.* We hear the lack of *natural* attraction.

The default attractions of these straight people *are* toward the gender they married, but neither spouse always *naturally* desires a mind/body/spirit connection with their spouse.

Is attraction really our issue?

Is my lack of attraction toward men what makes our marriage impossible? Or is it that *all* of our default attractions are toward *self,* and selfishness is what makes all of our marriages impossible?

I want . . . I need . . . You give me . . . we say.

• • •

What is the purpose of marriage?

Let's back it up: What is the purpose of life?

Well, as image bearers of a holy God, we are called to bear his image—serve as a visible picture of God—to the rest of the world (Genesis 1:26). We do this when we love each other, forgive each other, and work with one another in tandem with the Holy Spirit to bring restoration to a broken world (Matthew 6:10).

God is one, and we look like him when we are one with him, one within ourselves, and with each other. Then, we invite others into oneness with God. When people look at us, they are supposed to get a sense of the One who made them too. As they see a representation of God and feel a hunger for him, we are to declare him as the One all of our souls crave. In our image bearing, we are to point to Jesus. We are called to make disciples in our living and in our verbal invitations. We are to tell fellow image bearers that there is a Rescuer for our restless souls (Matthew 28:19; Romans 10:14).

So, if the purpose of being human is to point to God and, in so doing, point to Jesus as our rescuer, what is the purpose of marriage?

To point to God.

When a man and woman are united as one through marriage, we become a metaphor of "the way Christ and the church are one" (Ephesians 5:32). Marriage points to both the future and present reality that Jesus Christ wants to marry us, the church. Married people embody the gospel. Married people embody Jesus' embodied, sacrificial, one-flesh love for us in their sacrificial, one-flesh love for one another.

It is a great mystery.

The mystery is not what I've heard joked about at marriage events: A man and a woman grow attracted to each other, fall madly in love, hormones trick them into marriage, and putting a ring on it makes lust Christian-legal. But surprise! They're in a covenant now (and God hates divorce), so they have to figure out how to get along until they're dead.

No. Attraction is not the mystery. Falling in love is not the mystery. The great mystery is that *Christ wants to be one with us!* Marriage simply and profoundly illustrates this incredible reality to an aching world.

"God is infinitely *other,* infinitely *different* from his creation. And yet this infinitely different Creator does not hold himself aloof," Christopher West writes. "God wants to be *one* with his creation. God wants to *unite* with his creation. God wants to *marry* his creation."[1] God wants to marry us! This desire for divinity's oneness with creation is the theme of the whole Bible—from the first marriage in Genesis (2:21-24) to the final marriage in Revelation (19:6-9).

The purpose of marriage, then, is to tangibly demonstrate God's marriage proposal to us to our spouse and to the world. He is "the one." He is our lover. He is our savior. Jesus laid down his life to be one with us, so we must lay down our lives to be one with each other. "Like a bridegroom Christ went forth from his chamber," Saint Augustine said. "[Jesus] came to the marriage-bed of the cross, and there in mounting it, he consummated his marriage . . . and joined himself to [his Bride] forever."[2]

• • •

People say our marriage is impossible. They are right.

But so is yours.

My natural default is toward disunity with Matt, and his default is disunity with me.

Your natural default is toward disunity with your spouse.

And yet God calls us married folk to love him and to make disciples *as one.*[3]

Our marriages *feel* impossible. But they aren't. Nothing is impossible with God.

My natural default is toward disunity with the church as we press into The Marriage with Christ.

Matt's natural default is toward disunity with the church as we press into The Marriage with Christ.

Every person's natural default is disunity with the church as we press into The Marriage with Christ.

And yet God calls us to make disciples *as one*—to be unified (John 17:20-21).

The Marriage *feels* impossible. But it isn't. Nothing is impossible with God.

• • •

Before we begin this impossible-made-possible story, we have some words for a few specific kinds of readers.

People who are single. You might well be thinking, "Oh no, not another book about marriage." We have found that we are equally as passionate about singleness as we are about marriage and are committed to exhorting the church every time we speak on marriage to see singleness as we believe Jesus does. Married or single— these are the modes in which we undertake the mission to make disciples (1 Corinthians 7:35). One is not better than the other; they're just different—different modes and different metaphors.

When we married people love each other well, we serve as a metaphor to single people for how God wants to become one with them. When single people love Jesus well and have a beautiful relationship with the church body, they serve as a metaphor to us for how we will all be in eternity. Although this book focuses on marriage, we haven't and won't forget you, our incredible single friends.

People who disagree with us theologically when it comes to marriage. If you believe God's design for marriage and sexuality includes marriage for people of the same sex, we just want to say that we see you. We understand that this marriage conversation is personal, painful, and precious to you and that our very writing of this book may be offensive. We don't want to hurt you or those you love, but while we may have written the words in this book, we didn't write the words in the Bible. We are simply doing our best to live out our biblical beliefs and write about how that works practically in our marriage.

We have studied this "What does the Bible say about marriage?" question. The more we have studied, the more we are simultaneously convinced that God's design for marriage is between a man and woman and the more we are wrecked with God's compassion for those who disbelieve it. Theology makes us stronger yet softer.

This book you hold in your hands is not going to make a direct argument for biblical marriage. Instead, we are going to show you how two people live out the argument for biblical marriage. However, we will offer you one simple argument and then refer you to other resources.

When the Pharisees question Jesus about adultery in Matthew 19:3-5, Jesus says, "Haven't you read . . . that from the beginning 'God made them male and female.' . . . This explains why a man leaves his father and mother and is joined to his wife, and the two are united into one."

In this passage, Jesus links the creation of male and female ("male and female he created them" found in Genesis 1:27) to the one-flesh union ("the two will become one flesh" found in Genesis 2:24 NIV). So what is a one-flesh union according to Jesus here? It is a uniting of "the two." Which two? Two humans? Two people who love each other? No—man and wife, male and female. According to the Bible, a one-flesh union (what we call marriage) is a uniting of male and female.

Our favorite books to continue the conversation about biblical marriage—and our favorite marriage books in general—are Preston Sprinkle's *People to Be Loved,* Tim and Kathy Keller's *The Meaning of Marriage,* Christopher West's *Theology of the Body for Beginners,* and Francis and Lisa Chan's *You and Me Forever.* Laurie serves on the board of directors for Preston's Center for Faith, Sexuality & Gender, which offers many great resources that dive into biblical support for one man and one woman in a covenant, one-flesh union for life serving as the definition of marriage. In particular, the pastoral paper, "15 Reasons for the Affirming View and 15 Responses," is quite helpful for unpacking the arguments.

Our hope is that if you choose to read this—even if you disagree with us theologically—you will at least see we did our best job to share the grit and the glory of it. We are honest. Brutally so.

People who have experienced trauma. This conversation brings us to a trigger warning of sorts. As a licensed therapist, I, Matt, get that some people may not be ready to hear all of what we share in this book. We talk about trauma. And as someone who has experienced trauma, I, Laurie, get that there were seasons in my life when I could not have read something like this. We are not needlessly graphic, but we are honest and we share about the sexual assault I endured as a child. However, we will not take you to those times and let you suffer there. We want to point you to redemption and—we hope—specific ways in which you can walk away from the scenes if you have faced trauma yourself.

This book explores two major areas in Laurie's life: trauma and her attractions to the same sex. We need to say clearly and up front that we do not believe trauma *causes* same-sex attractions. Additionally, just because people experience attractions to the same sex does not mean they have also experienced trauma. These two things just happen to both be present in Laurie's story, but not everyone who has experienced one will also experience the other.

People in mixed-orientation marriages like ours. For those of you in a marriage like ours, we pray that you feel seen—even though your specific journey is unique. We pray that you experience hope, as opposed to the often-dismal foreshadowing Google offers you if you search for answers about mixed-orientation marriages. We pray that you feel seen by the church because straight couples read about our journey and are challenged by our story of an impossible marriage.

Straight couples in the church who want to understand the marriage conversation better. This brings us to the last group we want to address: straight couples. We are so grateful you are reading this. This marriage book is definitely for you.

Why? After taking surveys of couples like us, we believe we have found the greatest *unique* challenge in marriages like ours.

It's not sex—you straight couples have your issues here too.

It's not lust—it's hard to find a straight marriage unaffected by porn at some point.

It's not theological quandaries—all believers face these.

Our greatest unique issue is that we don't feel we can take our specific sex, lust, and theological struggles *to you*. It can be challenging to find a theologically orthodox friend, therapist, or pastor who is also sensitive to our situation. Our struggles are so similar to straight couples, and yet many of us feel our greatest issue is our isolation. We feel we cannot take our similar-but-slightly-different pain to you.

Why do we feel that way? Some of us have. And many responses have been amazing. (You'll read about a couple of examples in the chapters to follow.) But some reactions are not always great. Both of us have received the following as marriage advice:

"Just have more sex with him—that will make it better."

"Just pray."

"You should leave him and find a wife."

"You should leave her and find a better wife."

"Serve her by cleaning the kitchen, and you'll get sex in the bedroom."

"I'll pray for you"—said with terrified eyes. There was no follow-up conversation.

Walking through our version of an impossible marriage has taught us something: We, the church, often do not know how to wisely advise each other when it comes to marriage, period. We are not focused on serving as a metaphor of The Marriage between Christ and the church. We are not focused on dying to our selves and pursuing oneness with our spouses in order to show the world a picture of how Jesus died for us and how we are to die daily to be one with him.

Instead, we're often focused on communication tactics, sexual gratification, and trying to "fall back in love" or "get the spark back" again. These platitudes aren't ultimately helpful for any marriage. We need something more than these airy things. We need the truth. We need to stare at The Marriage.

We all do—no matter our marriage type.

We pray that this book—positioned in the middle of the current massive cultural deconstruction of marriage on the whole—will serve as a wake-up call, prompting the entire church to ask: What is the purpose of marriage? Why have we so emphasized sex, communication, and "falling in love" over the metaphor of marriage? Is it truly helping any of us?

Dear straight couples, as you read this, we hope you'll ask yourselves, "Can I relate to this version of an impossible marriage? How is my own marriage equally impossible? How is it equally possible?" If you find you can relate, it will not only de-isolate couples like us, it will also further unify the church because married people will not be staring at their spouses—we will all be staring at God.

All marriages are impossible.

This is simply our story of the impossible-made-possible because of Jesus.

ONE

WHAT DO YOU WANT?

[Jesus] is always to be found in the thickest part of the battle.
When the wind blows cold He always takes the bleak side of the
hill. The heaviest end of the cross lies ever on His shoulders. If
He bids us carry a burden, He carries it also. If there is anything
that is gracious, generous, kind, and tender, yea lavish and super-
abundant in love, you always find it in Him.

CHARLES SPURGEON

LAURIE

"What do you want?"

A friend asked me the question assuming she knew the answer: You *want* Matt. You *want* to be with him.

Did I? Did I *want* that?

I packed the question into my suitcase of warm clothes as I headed out into the Michigan snow. Our mentor had gifted both Matt and me with separate silent retreats, and it was my turn.

What do you want?

Over the previous year, I hadn't given myself permission to ask such a question; I simply lived in our fractured home.

When our second daughter was born, a repressed memory came to the surface. It was a blurry one that included sexual assault by a stranger when I was very young. Something about the birth of Juliette jolted my brain into remembering the birth of my younger brother, which happened around the time of the assault. My present life woke up my past life. The memory came back in unwanted flashes paired with panic attacks. I went into a near-catatonic state whenever Matt walked into certain rooms. Matt was not my attacker, but his maleness reminded me of him.

I dug into my spiritual and emotional toolbox to try to solve this ridiculous issue. ("Hello, I love Matt!") But no matter how much I tried, the memory only gripped me tighter. None of my favorite tools were working: prayer, books, counseling.

As time wore on, the memory intertwined itself with my sexual orientation, intensifying the situation. *Matt is scary,* the memory whispered. *But you don't like men anyway,* my desires for women said.

Since I was very young, I experienced attraction toward my same gender. Girls were interesting, and boys were . . . like my five brothers. They were fun to play G.I. Joe and LEGO with, but they did not draw my eyes or attention. What began as a heart flutter around certain girls turned into a secret same-sex relationship in college.

Matt and I met while I was in such a relationship. It became clear he was interested in me as more than a friend. "Hold up," I said. "You have no idea what's going on with me." I didn't know what to say to him. I didn't identify as gay or someone who experiences same-sex attractions (SSA), or any of the words you hear today. I didn't even *consider* myself gay or SSA. I just liked girls, I wasn't sexually attracted to men, and I was in a same-sex relationship.

Even though I was in quite a bit of denial about my attractions toward women, there was something about this Matt guy that drew me toward him in the midst of my sexual questioning. Our hearts ached over the same things, laughed about the same things, and desired the same thing: to care for the lost and the broken. I was not initially physically attracted to him, but I was drawn to him in other ways, which led to physical attraction.

We started out as good friends. When Matt made his intentions clear, I told him to pray until I was ready to share "what was going on with me." When I did, he said he saw me no differently—and he didn't. Charlotte Brontë said, "The soul, fortunately, has an interpreter—often an unconscious but still a faithful interpreter—in the eye."[1] Matt's eyes revealed the truth of his words.

We started dating, and about a month into our dating relationship I broke up with my not-technically-girlfriend girlfriend. (That season was as messy as it sounds.) Matt and I experienced a sweet relationship for about a year, but then I broke up with him too. "God said no," I told him.

I believe God prompted this move because I needed some major heart work before talking about marriage—which we were. "I don't want to get married," I journaled during class one day. "But I do want to marry Matt." By that I meant I knew that if we were going to get married, it would not be stereotypical—a doting wife and a take-the-reins husband. But I also saw we could be partners as we served God together. We could be friends who made each other laugh, had each other's back, and worshiped Jesus together.

We did not imagine that even those minimal (though idealistic) dreams would fall like sand through our fingers eight years later.

But if we had gotten married before our breakup? I don't think we would have lasted a year. I would have cheated or . . . something. But while we were apart, God connected me with a counselor and fellow Christian who God used to take my focus off of both women and men and place it on Jesus.

I became joyful. Hopeful. I was ready to move to one of the US coasts, earn my doctorate, and become a happy English professor while married to Jesus.

But then God called me to an earthly marriage. "I have someone for you," he whispered.

"No," I said back. I was always very honest with God. "God, you know my sexual attractions are toward women, but I am willing to surrender those to you daily. I just want to be married to you."

"But I want you to live out your mission of making disciples as a married woman," he said.

I paused. "Fine. But you better pick him out for me because that is stressful."

I didn't think Matt would enter the picture again. God had said no before.

In his kindness, God brought Matt back. Through our breakup, God seemed to push pause on my love for Matt, gutted my perspective, called me to marriage, unpaused my love for Matt, and then put me in front of him. I reached out to Matt to "talk about something" in an email, and so we met at a Wendy's over chocolate Frosties. (It was all very romantic.) "I think I still love you," I said as my shake melted.

"I'm about to meet up with a girl I liked before I liked you," he said, slowly chewing on a French fry.

"Okay," I said, glaring at God.

"I'll let you know," Matt said.

Then God struck Matt's house with lightning.

Not kidding. Matt was watching sports on TV in the middle of a thunderstorm and *zzzzap*. It went dark. Matt was fine, but the strike fried all of the electronic devices in his house. As a poor, just-graduated-college guy, he didn't have the money to replace it all, let alone begin to pursue this other woman (who lived in another state at the time).

Instead, he visited his parents. "So, I think Laurie is back in the picture?" he told them.

"Laurie? We love Laurie!" They knew my story—all of it—and loved me and us through it.

"But I'm not good enough for her," he replied. This was a theme of his life and the real reason he was hesitant to pursue me.

"You don't have to be perfect, son," his dad said. "Just be teachable."

One month later we were engaged. Three months after that we were married and ready to take on the world in the mode we are called to make disciples.

But we also weren't ready. We didn't understand that yet. The first honeymoon years were sweet—we laughed often together. Then came the dark years of Matt's addiction to porn, followed by a year of light after he repented. And then, suddenly, our marriage movie cut to black.

Eight years in, after our second daughter's birth, I couldn't be in the same room with Matt without my entire body stiffening with fear bathed in rage. I felt like a jaguar. "Get away from me," I growled. We could not be physically close in any capacity for over a year and a half. My childhood memory saw Matt as a threat, and my sexual orientation offered what seemed to be a peaceful, freeing escape.

Matt was still the amazing man I married—even better. I had watched him grow in mind, body, and spirit throughout the near-decade of knowing him. And I had grown too. But after the memory resurfaced, the easy laughter and friendship that had permeated our dating relationship became harder and harder to find. There were moments, hours, and even days when we felt a springtime thaw, but then something else would trigger me and a blizzard would refreeze my heart.

The frozen, snowy roads matched the state of my heart as I drove to the silent retreat center.

What do I want?

"I need God to wake me up about marriage," I told a friend before leaving. "I need him to download something fresh . . ." I couldn't finish the sentence like I wanted to: ". . . so that I want to stay married." Christians don't say those things. They only think them quietly and announce them publicly to an uproar after building up files of reasons to leave. I had a lot of files.

I did *want* something fresh from God. I felt I needed it.

After unloading my bags into my room, I bundled up to take a walk in the woods. The winter sun cut through the trees. Snow

sparkled, but only my eyes noticed. My icy soul couldn't respond
in worship to the God who made it.

A mile into my walk, I felt the urge to run. *Run, run, run.* I had
been running for exercise all winter, and I wanted my muscles
to burn with the faster pace. *I want to feel something. Anything.
Even pain.* Maybe pain could melt my heart. There were times I
stared at Matt across the icy tundra in our home and willed my
heart to thaw by seeing his sad face. *Maybe if I see him in enough
agony, I'll want to change, to stay, to work harder.* But even though
Matt was kind toward me in the midst of turmoil, and even
though he sometimes bared his own raw, shredded soul, it did
not tap into my empathy. If anything, I bundled myself up further
to protect my own aching heart.

"Where are you going?" I heard in a still, small voice.

"I want to get to the next thing," I said.

"What is the next thing?" it said.

"I don't know." I was afraid of finding out. *Leaving him?*

Back at the retreat center, I signed up for an hour-long session
with a spiritual director. The woman was a kind, earthy type who
likely listened to talk radio and ate vegan from her own garden.
After she asked a few insightful questions, I shared with her how
I came to find a new perspective on marriage. "It's been really
hard," I said, making vague allusions to having difficulty connecting with my husband. She quoted the Christian mystics, dug
into some Scripture about how "from death comes life," and said,
"Sticking it out can bring gifts and even greater joy."

I thanked her, but I received none of her words. There was a
lingering question in the back of my mind. "What if she knew?"
What would she say if she knew that my default sexual attraction
was toward women and not my husband? How would her advice
change? Some friends had offered solutions before, many of
them matching the advice I could easily find on the internet: I
don't have to die to myself. My type of marriage is too hard.
Sticking it out won't bring joy. My metaphorical death doesn't
bring life—only more death. In fact, it is itself a kind of assault.

Or maybe I was reading her wrong. She might have swung to the opposite extreme: Pray more. Have lots of sex with your spouse. Just do it. Force yourself. Submit yourself. It'll fix you. But such an answer would have only been another kind of assault to my soul.

Where was the middle road? Where was the one that upheld the covenant and the purpose of marriage to point to Jesus but also held my experience with tenderness?

Wrapping myself in a blanket, I plopped into a sunbathed chair in front of a corner window. For the next three hours I wrestled with God.

What do I want? I looked out at the still-sparkling snow and journaled.

> I'm on the edge of a cliff. Do I stay or do I go?
> Do I want to be married?
> Do I want to be married to Matt?
> No. To be honest? No. I don't. I'd love to be his friend.
> Is that not enough? Is friendship not enough?

I thought of the spiritual director and what I assumed her advice would have been if I had been completely honest with her. *Just leave. You have a free get-out-of-marriage card because of your sexual orientation.*

> Do I get a free pass to exit this relationship because I'm attracted to the same gender?
> Do the death-to-self rules change for me because I am who I am?
> Is there a different set of guidelines for me?
> The world says, "Yes." The world says, "Start over. Be like other 'liberated lesbians.' Be best friends with your husband, but fall in love with a woman. Finally, be you and express yourself the way you need to."
> That's very tempting. It's what I want.
> But is it what I need?

A prompting encouraged me to flip my well-worn Bible to Psalm 37. I had a sense God was directing me to a certain verse. *Take delight in the LORD, / and he will give you your heart's desires* (v. 4).

Is my heart's desire a committed relationship with a woman? Is my heart's desire to be in love? What is my heart's desire?

Maybe I don't know my heart. Maybe I don't know what it needs. Maybe I don't know what to feed it. Like my kids who think their cravings for sugar are going to satisfy, perhaps I think some human sugar will satisfy.

I looked over at the woods where I had recently run. I recalled the still, small voice asking me where I was going. "I want to get to the next thing," I had said.

I quieted my unruly will and went back to that moment. The voice kept speaking. "No, don't go to the next thing. Don't run away. Pause for a minute. Come with me."

In my mind's eye I saw myself sitting on a throne, which I took to be the judgment seat. Instead of deciding good and evil, I knew my role was to decide what would come next in my life. "Do you think you know what is best for you?" the voice asked. I could see who was speaking now. It was an angel. One of God's representatives—all bright, shining, and peaceful but also serious.

"Um, yes?" I said hesitantly at first, then garnered more courage. "Yes. I do know what is best for me." I looked in front of the judgment seat. There were a million buttons and slides that made it look like a DJ sound booth. I knew my job was to pick the right buttons in the right sequence to choose my next right step. I instinctively knew that the wrong buttons would yield devastating results. My finger hovered over one, but I could foresee it would usher in the death of my children. I put my finger over another but sensed it would cause a fire that would tear through blocks of buildings. *There has to be a less intense sequence to choose,* I thought. But I couldn't find it. I didn't know the rules for this machine.

"I can't pick," I told the angel at last.

"Who can?" he asked. "Who do you trust with the controls?" Of course, I knew the right answer, but the way he phrased it kept me from rolling my eyes. He didn't ask, "Do you trust God?" He asked, "Who do you trust to lead your life?"

He went on. "Wouldn't you rather give the controls to someone who made you, made your world, knows the past and the future, created everyone else, is completely unbiased and yet biased toward all of you equally? Not only did he tell you how to live well, he lived it himself, and made a path for us to live it through himself. Wouldn't you rather have him choose what is best for your life?"

"Yes! But, God . . . *but, God!*" I stopped talking to the angel and turned my conversation to his boss. I knew he heard me—us. I knew he was involved in this whole stupid thing. "It is so hard! Not pretend hard but like *really hard.* Not Disney-movie hard but *ripping-my-heart-apart hard!*"

"I know, Laurie. I know. I wrote it, and I've walked it . . . with you. I have experienced the devastation of the broken world and the havoc it has had on your soul with you. I have never left you."

He was good, but I didn't let him crack me. "But, God! I would have so many more friends! I would have the type of intimate connection I want."

"So, that's it, Laurie? It's about sex? It's about pleasure—pleasure I made in the first place—that you want to take out of my design? You want to eat the apple I said no to? You want *that* tree?"

That made me pause. "But the world! The world, God! The world says, 'I'll love you if you come out. I won't fight you. I will *champion* you.' I am so tired, God. So tired of fighting."

"They said that to me, too: 'We will love you if you become king! We won't kill you if you just stop saying you are God. We will champion you if you take over the way we want you to.'"

"STOP IT. Stop. Just stop. You don't get it. You don't know *this* type of pain. This is different. *And you are Jesus!*"

I waited for him to fight me. "You aren't even going to respond to that, are you?" Nothing. He didn't. "God, I know what I want . . ."

"And where does getting what you want lead?" There he was. "Where will it take you, Laurie? Walk it all the way down the trail . . ."

I wrote:

If I was to divorce Matt:

The good: I would be free. I would find someone who loved me and with whom I could have the intimacy I desire. I would be championed by some friends and some Christians. I'd feel treasured. I'd feel like a queen.

The hard: My kids. I wouldn't want to lose them. I wouldn't want to confuse them. I'd want them to have Matt in their life. I don't know how long the physical aspect with someone new would last. I don't know if the person would love me for me. I don't know how long it would take until I would be frustrated with her neediness.

I wouldn't be championed by everyone. I would be despised by some. I would probably become bitter toward them. I would lose some dear friends. If they ignored my pleas that I was still the same person, I would probably write them off as haters who don't understand. Or I would try to convince them that this is the right way, the Christian way.

I would feel desired. I would feel wanted.

I would remember the days I felt like a queen with Matt: How he looked at me. How he treasured me. I would miss his strength. I would miss his masculinity. His shoulders. I've always liked his shoulders—to me they exemplify strength. A covering.

I would probably cover the matching tattoo we have.

Would I go to hell?

That's a sobering question. But not enough. Or is it? Is it?

I wanted to be done thinking. Done writing. Done wrestling. I sent Matt a text, "I'm not doing well." Perhaps this would warn him of what was to come.

But God wasn't done with me. "Laurie, do you want to silence the Holy Spirit's presence in you?"

I knew what God was alluding to. It was from the book of Jude, which I hardly ever read but happened to read the day before. Certain verses popped out to me as if they were radioactive:

> But you, my dear friends, must remember what the apostles of our Lord Jesus Christ predicted. They told you that in the last times there would be scoffers whose purpose in life is to satisfy their ungodly desires. These people are the ones who are creating divisions among you. They follow their natural instincts because they do not have God's Spirit in them. (Jude 17-19)

There are those who follow their *natural instincts* toward *ungodly desires* because they *don't have God's Spirit in them.*

If I followed my natural instincts for a woman, would I not have God's Spirit in me?

"Fine. Let's walk that down the trail of possibilities," I thought. Everything was on the table. Even my faith. "What does your Spirit actually give me?" I knew I was playing with fire, but in that moment I did not care.

I stared ahead toward this question.

As I did, I suddenly felt sharply cold and terrified. I did not feel like I tumbled into a black hole, but that I was one. I felt like I had just siphoned life out of everything around me but was still hollow. I was dark, freezing, and to-my-cells lonely. My bones were lead, and I could not breathe.

The moment ended, and I gasped.

What just happened?

I believe God allowed me to experience a fraction of hell for two microseconds. Not even the full thing, just a breath of it. It took my breath away and left me shaking.

I looked outside at the sunshine while I panted. I wanted the sun to warm me. *Did God just let me experience a fraction of life devoid of him?* My eyes were wide as I processed what that meant.

The Holy Spirit isn't just some Jiminy Cricket guide in our lives. He is all-comforting, all-wise, and the only source of peace. He is God on earth now. If I followed what I wanted . . . it would lead to a life empty of true comfort, wisdom, and peace. It could lead to hell, a restless separation from God, always seeking but never finding that peace.[2]

"Do you want to silence the Holy Spirit's presence in you?" He asked again.

"No."

"Then follow me. Trust me. Come and die."

• • •

The next morning, I woke up at 5 a.m. to a swirling snowstorm.

Knowing I had received what God had for me for the weekend, I packed up my things and jumped in the car before the sun rose. Gone were the sunshine and diamond snow. Gone, too, was my wrestling with staying or leaving Matt. I was resolved.

I had *not* decided to go home, kiss Matt's face, and surrender to a straight marriage. But I was resolved to God being God. I surrendered to him, and I wanted what *he wanted.* This meant I wanted the life he called me to, the one I covenanted before God and others: a life with Matt and our kids.

I had no idea how he would fix our crumbling marriage. I had no idea whether Matt and I would ever be close again physically.

All I knew was that I did not get a free pass to exit the relationship. There was not a different rule book for me. The death-to-self gospel was equally good news for me as it was for the straightest person I knew.

My arms shook as my car cut through the predawn darkness, the flakes falling fast. I was not quivering from fear of the blizzard but from my very real encounter with a holy God. My arms shook, and my heart felt raw from a surgery no one could see. I needed some recovery.

"God, what will you give me in exchange for this surrender?" I asked while my car slowly ascended and descended the wooded hills. I was still self-focused. I hoped God would tell me something about how we aren't going to simply survive but thrive.

"Laurie? You will hear my Spirit even more. You will be able to discern even more clearly."

I guessed that was nice. His words were not what I *wanted*, but perhaps they were what I *needed*.

I had a lot to discern.

I had a lot to learn.

• • •

MATT

Laurie texted me from her retreat: "I'm not doing well."

I knew immediately that this was not a reference to a general malaise about life. We had been in severe marital pain for over a year, and she had become increasingly distant. This avoidance was not the same type I leaned toward in suffering, which was distant, detached—what Laurie called "Planet Matt." Planet Matt was a landing place for my mind to think about the ridiculous, such as what to do in a real-life velociraptor attack, or to add to my list of dad jokes.

Laurie's type of avoidance included hostility, which felt like invisible knives pointed at me. If I tried to get close to her in any way—with jokes, conversation, or (heaven forbid, for her) physically—the claws came out. It was often only with a look, but it shredded me.

When she texted that single line, I went back to my word for the year: steadfast. I had chosen it after much prayer, and it seemed to be a theme for this year of suffering. Just don't move. Don't get close to her. Don't get too far away.

But pray, Matt, I heard in a still, small voice after reading her text. *Pray for Laurie.*

Our oldest daughter, Gwyn, couldn't sleep. I carried my burden of prayer into her room as I comforted her. "When is Mama coming home?" she wailed.

"Don't worry," I said. "Mama will be home tomorrow." I rubbed her back, wondering to myself, *Will she?* I didn't know.

As I fell asleep, I tried not to escape to my own planet but instead to stay in a space of prayer. *Help, God. Help Laurie. Please, help our marriage.*

People have asked us many times how we chose to get married when we knew Laurie's orientation. There were two things that helped me pre-marriage: One, Laurie's attraction toward women didn't threaten me. If she left me for a man, I'd feel like there was something about me that wasn't manly enough. If she left me for another woman, I could never be a woman, so . . . there. That was a competition I couldn't participate in.

The second thing that helped was that Laurie always said, "I'm not attracted to men, but I am attracted to Matt." That phrase felt good for many years—until we slammed our heads against her level of *un-attraction* toward me. The uncovered memory brought it to the surface for her. As the past became clearer, so did Laurie's realization that she had been detaching from any physical parts of our marriage from the start. Days before leaving on her silent retreat, she had told me, "I never wanted to kiss you—even on our wedding day."

We had our first kiss after we said our vows. Laurie told me she wanted to wait until then (if she ever got married) because she didn't want "to replace one lust with another." She had just broken up with her girlfriend and didn't want to numb out on hormones that can come with physical connection to anyone. I believed her. She truly believed herself. But she buried a box deep inside her that held her desire to have physical connection with a man—her husband. I thought when we were married, we would open it and it would be filled with all sorts of desire-for-Matt-only treasures. She thought so too. But the box was empty. Neither of us really knew the truth while she detached her mind from her body for eight years.

I wanted her fixed. I hate even saying that, but the reality was I did not want this pain. I wanted my wife back. Or a new version of her? Or one that at least didn't resent me? I didn't want her straight—I knew her story when we married, but I wanted her to be "Matt attracted" as she had said so many times in the early years. I mostly wanted peace in our home. I encouraged her to seek counseling, but as a therapist I knew it was unwise to strongly exhort someone to go. They need to want it, and Laurie did not. Her heart was locked, and she held the keys.

She also held the keys to the car that could drive her away from us forever.

Pray, Matt.

The next morning, I threw hats and snow pants on our girls so that we could play in the winter wonderland outside. As I bundled them up, I was surprised to hear the garage open. "I'm home!" Laurie said, smiling hugely. She hugged the girls, and even hugged me. My nervous, racing heart slowed as I saw—what was that? *Peace? A shred of genuine joy?* I kept my questions quiet as we romped around in the snow together, laughing. She tackled me several times, and we laughed and played like we hadn't in many months.

When we put the kids down for a nap, Laurie sat me down at the kitchen table.

"Should I be scared?" I asked. Maybe this would be when she let the axe fall. Play first, leave later.

"Not really," she said, but her face was serious. "You're not in trouble."

She told me she had been wrestling with leaving. She had never said those words aloud before. Her hostile detachment from our marriage had been a quiet one. Still, I wasn't shocked. God had prepared me.

"If I want to be with God," she said, "then I want to be with you." I didn't hear her toss the words out in some sort of angry resolve. She seemed on an unsure foundation, but at least there was a foundation and the start of peace.

"That's surprisingly comforting," I said, sighing, playing with the crumbs on the table. "I know that in the battle between me and a woman, a woman would win. But in the battle between women and God, God would win." I knew Laurie. She might wrestle for months or years with God, but at the end of the day she would never quit him.

The axe fell the next day. She let me read her back-and-forth conversation with God, and I felt the lacerations on my chest as—for the first time—I read the depth of her un-like for me. Her journal did not hold the genuinely sweet moments in our relationship: her choosing me, our friendship, and her desire to follow God. Instead, this journal entry revealed all the darkest thoughts including her total and complete lack of physical desire for me.

It hurt deeply.

We needed help. I needed help. Unfortunately, my prayers in that season were not, "Help me." My prayers were, "Help her." I wanted *Laurie* better so that I could have peace and so that we could have at least some kind of a physical connection. I felt justified in how I was petitioning God.

But oh, how much I had to learn. Not about Laurie's same-sex attractions or her assault but about my own idolatry of sex. In my mind, I was a normal, red-blooded, respectful, heterosexual Christian guy, but I thought sex was what I *needed*—not just what I wanted.

Those of us men who grow up as—well, men—learn we are very visually, sexually driven especially around the time of junior high. And it is true. Louann Brizendine, a neuropsychiatrist and the author of *The Female Brain* and *The Male Brain*, has noted how the part of the brain dedicated to sexual pursuit is 2.5 times larger in men than women. Furthermore, in their teens, young men produce twenty to twenty-five times more testosterone than in pre-adolescence. "If testosterone were beer," she said, "a 9-year-old boy would be getting the equivalent of a cup a day. But a 15-year-old would be getting the equivalent of nearly two gallons a day."[3]

So, what are Christian young men told when they are hitting that two-gallon-a-day drinking phase? Sex is good. You're going to want it. But don't. Just wait until marriage. *And then what?* Well, the assumption to even the Christian male brain is "My wife and I will have lots of sex and be happy." Oh, there were some caveats too: "Men, sex starts in the kitchen. Love and serve your wife there, and you will be rewarded with sex." We exchange service for sex. We exchange heart connection for sex. But what is the end goal? Sex. What is the focus? Sex. What is the commodity we are trading? Sex.

It's Christianized, but the idol is still there: sex as a need.

In my counseling practice I meet with many types of couples. If there is a sexual issue in the marriage (either the husband or wife desiring more sexual intimacy than the other), do you know what the most quoted set of verses is?

> The husband should fulfill his wife's sexual needs, and the wife should fulfill her husband's needs. The wife gives authority over her body to her husband, and the husband gives authority over his body to his wife.
>
> Do not deprive each other of sexual relations, unless you both agree to refrain from sexual intimacy for a limited time so you can give yourselves more completely to prayer. Afterward, you should come together again so that Satan won't be able to tempt you because of your lack of self-control. (1 Corinthians 7:3-5)

"See? My wife should be with me more often!" the finger-pointing husband says. "See? My husband should want me more!" the finger-pointing wife says. But they don't notice the verb is reflexive. "Do not deprive each other," Paul says. Not, "Make sure the other is not depriving you." He's saying, "Check *yourself*."

These finger-pointing conversations become more complex and shame-laden in marriages where the male/female stereotypes break down. If the husband is having a hard time connecting with his wife (or even having any sort of desire), she can cross her arms in a huff and say, "It's not supposed to be like this. I am the woman! I shouldn't want it more than the man!" He feels shamed and the desire to be close to her disappears further into his own self-hatred.

For a woman, having trouble with a lack of desire to be physically close to her husband can stem from a number of places. She can feel intimidated by her husband's masculinity and his sexual pursuits can be seen as demands. This does not draw a woman's heart to a man; it terrifies or repulses her. Laurie felt this and cowered or became jaguar-like—even if all I wanted was to sit next to her.

Although I saw these demanding, finger-pointing attitudes in my practice, even though I gave talks on the idolatry of sex and marriage, I did not have the mirror up close enough to my face to see my own idol-worshiping reflection.

Sex is not a need—even in marriage. Sex is fruit. It is a gift for covenanted couples. It is a gospel metaphor within the gospel metaphor of marriage. It is something to be used to worship God, not to be demanded.

I did not know that yet. I had a lot to learn.

TWO

A HALF STEP

Why would anyone be shocked to hear of my struggles
with past and present sin when the Cross already
told them I am a desperately sinful person?

MILTON VINCENT

LAURIE

I let Matt read the back-and-forth between God and me in the early morning of the day after I returned. He didn't speak to me again until later that evening.

"Why did you have me read that?" he asked. "What good did you think it would do?"

I knew what it was like to live out my role in the marriage; he didn't. I knew how difficult the sexual connection had been; he didn't. I knew I had been detaching; he didn't.

Now Matt learned my level of un-attraction toward him— even as I woke up to it myself.

After I decided to stay married, it was as if a lamp was lit and showed me where I was.

I was entertaining a lot of what-ifs: *What if you left? What if you didn't have to fight the world anymore? What if you got what you wanted? How many people would love you? How would your life be so much better?* These were just ideas (no plans were made), but I treasured each *what-if.* They were like secret candy I pulled out and sampled when I felt empty.

I wondered if there would be a day when I would cheat on Matt. I could see myself wandering with a woman for a while and then feeling convicted enough to come back. I even envisioned my repentance—feeling genuinely sorry for what I'd done—but *then* I would know. *Then* I would be all-in with Matt. We would look back together on that terrible season, but I would grow from it, love him more, and get the uncertainty out of my system.

On my silent retreat, the Holy Spirit highlighted the secret *what-if* candy I hoarded. *Choose. Are you going to keep hiding and treasuring those questions? Or will you choose me?*

I chose God. And because I chose God, I chose the covenant marriage he had for me.

After I decided, I could see clearly that my what-if thinking is called adultery. Jesus said, "Anyone who even looks at a woman with lust has already committed adultery with her in his heart" (Matthew 5:28). It is the look, the thought, the treasuring of secret questions, and the moving toward sin that condemns us.

And yet God gives grace freely. He declares us guilty but not condemned because he takes the penalty (John 8:10-11). His grace is a free gift for the world, but it cost him. If we choose to receive this gift, we must consider the price tag of his life.

The day Matt read the journals between God and me, we did not speak until after the kids were in bed. During those silent hours, I reflected on what my seemingly innocuous sin had cost Jesus. Having a sexual orientation that did not naturally draw me to Matt did not let me off the hook. Just because I had been assaulted did not mean I had a right to wander. Somewhere along the way I had started to believe I had a *right* to sin and then that my thoughts weren't even sinful. At some point, I forgot that Jesus had to die for me.

I journaled repentance:

Oh, God, forgive me. There is a file system I have been creating with file titles like:
"Reasons I am gay and need to leave."

"Reasons to cheat."

"Reasons I don't have to give my whole heart to Matt."

"Reasons I am excluded from all the marriage verses."

I need to destroy this file cabinet. God, I can't burn it on my own. I need you to help me.

Not only had I been hoarding and treasuring my *what-ifs*, I had been filing evidence for me to live out the fantasy. *Help me, Jesus,* I prayed. Surrendering this fantasy future felt impossible.

Slowly, with the Holy Spirit empowering me, I opened up my hands. "Here. Take them. Take the *what-ifs*. Take all the files I have been hiding of secret reasons to leave. Forgive me, Jesus."

He did. So kindly. So gently—without shame or the backhand to the face I felt I deserved.

After that brief prayer, I felt surprisingly empty and sad. The fantasy world where I secretly lived had been a source of comfort to me in that season of suffering. I didn't have many comforts in those days.

But the *what-ifs*, the fantasies, the idols we cling to are not truly kind. They're killers. If they are not God's design, their only path is toward one of death.

Even though I knew that, even though I knew I had created a fantasy map strung together out of what-if questions, when it was gone, it left me with no next step. No trajectory. I felt hopeless. Before, at least I had a daydream; now I had . . . what? I felt empty and afraid.

"How do I do this, Jesus?" I asked.

"Dear one?" that still small voice whispered. "The only way you can turn from the fantasy—your desires—is to replace it with me. You need to trust me. Trust my heart for you. Trust my love is enough—not Matt's love—my love. Matt is a gift for you. I am enough for you."

"Okay, Jesus, okay," I said. "I will try." Even though I still felt empty, I took a stumbling half step forward.

• • •

"Can we talk?" I asked Matt after the girls were in bed. His eyes were pained, blankly staring into space as he sat on our toddler-worn couch. He nodded.

I fought the desire to run. My sin was now exposed but forgiven by Jesus, but Matt? Would he forgive me? I feared what he might say, mourned over what I had done, and fought the desire to cover my worry and sorrow with anger.

Anger is an easier emotion to feel than fear or sadness, but it is also less vulnerable. I mentally picked up my defensiveness and tossed it aside. I would not hide behind that mask. I would stay in a position of humble vulnerability and genuine sorrow.

Instead of running, I bought time by getting ready for bed—breathing deeply and praying the whole time. When I came back to the living room, Matt was still sitting on the couch in the same blank position. He was a man rejected, feeling unwanted and undesirable.

I fell down to my knees. I knew of no other suitable posture.

"Matt, I know it doesn't seem like it, but I am more committed to you than I have ever been." I wiped away a tear. "I am so sorry for my wandering heart and the depth of my fantasy. I have exposed my soul before you and this is my time of repentance."

Matt sat up from his defeated, slumped position at my allusion. Three years earlier, he had confessed a secret, five-year addiction to pornography. That was his "time of repentance." He noticed my intentional word choice.

"I'm committed to you even if you aren't," I said.

He looked down again and whispered, "I am."

"Well, good," I said, "but no matter what, I am in this." The void of the surrendered *what-ifs* wasn't as palpable now. I felt the Holy Spirit filling the empty places with a fresh wind. "At some point, I would like to hear from you how I can show you that I am all in. You did the same thing for me after you came forward with your secrets."

At the advice of a trusted counselor, I had written out my specific desires for Matt to demonstrate his loyalty post-porn confession. It included things like, "I want to see you reading the Word. I would like for you to be clean from porn for six months. I'd like you to find a Christian brother with whom you can share heart-to-heart about anything. Then, you will have my trust."

Trust is earned, not demanded. Jesus—the most trustworthy person—doesn't even demand trust from us. Instead, he calls, "If any of you wants to be my follower, you must give up your own way, take up your cross, and follow me" (Matthew 16:24). The key phrase here is, "If any of you wants." He doesn't say, "You have to, human robots." Jesus offers himself fully, invites us to join him in surrender to the Father's will, and asks us to join him on the mission to make disciples.

Matt did these three things and more. He has not looked at pornography since the day it came into the light. Now my darkness had come into the light, and I needed tangible ways to show him.

But first, forgiveness. I knew he could take days, months, or years to give it to me. However, he paused and looked me in the eye. "I forgive you, Laurie." He said each word as if pulling a fishhook from his gut. It hurt, but once it was out, there was raw peace. "I forgive you for the hiding, and I forgive you for the depth of the fantasy."

I breathed, not realizing I was holding it in while he spoke. "Thank you." I smiled and left him with his thoughts as I went to bed.

• • •

Matt shared some tangible ways to show him love in the following days. The first thing he asked was that I hug him when he came down the stairs in the morning.

Marriage counselors and experts offer four times of critical "touch points" during the day to help sustain a connection to your spouse.[1] The first is when you wake up, the next is when one or both of you leave for work, and the third is in those critical ninety seconds upon arriving home. That minute-and-a-half has been noted as the most important tone-setter for the rest of the day. An out-of-home worker must shed work worries and engage his or her partner with a smile and a hug. "I'm here. This is hard. But we're on the same team." The last important touch point is right before bed. The ideal form of touch is a hug or a kiss.

Some marriage counselors suggest that daily, passionate kissing can help keep couples connected. Daily, passionate kissing had a zero percent chance of happening in that season, and apart from some sort of major transformation, likely will not happen still. However, as I say to the people I mentor who are in mixed-orientation marriages like ours, "What steps are you comfortable taking? Do that and ask Jesus if you are ready to take one half-step more."

Could I hug Matt first thing in the morning? With the curtains closed so that even my subconscious didn't think someone could watch and judge me from outside? Yes, I could do that. To show Matt how much I truly loved him, for the sake of our marriage, to offer our kids an example of God's love for them, I could hug Matt.

And so, I began.

It felt awkward but not overly so. Strangely, after repenting and after recommitting to Matt, I wanted hug him. I went from bristling every time he walked into the room to being okay with an occasional embrace. My repentance turned my heart toward God, and God began turning my heart toward his will for my life—oneness with my husband.

Now, I need to say that this was the right time for such a shift. Before the silent retreat, I was not ready. Mentors in my life had pushed me toward this kind of physical touch before (I had pushed myself!), but it had been too fast. Too early. My heart was not ready. Rather than a half step from where I was, their recommendation was a four-step leap ahead.

Our timeline for healing often does not match God's. He is so much more patient than we are.

The second thing Matt asked of me was to share the reasons I like him. Our brains are constantly taking notes, creating files, and collecting data. I needed a collection bin for these thoughts. With my mind now void of *what-if* questions and reasons to leave, I wanted to fill it with something else. I began a tangible list I called, "Reasons I Love Matt" and kept it in the "Reminders" section of my phone. I shared it with Matt so that he could see it any time. I had been storing resentment for years; now it was time for kindness.

Hearing and reading the list of reasons helped Matt feel like I wanted to be with him, if not physically, at least as friends—like the old times. A few of the things I wrote were, "He loves decorating for Christmas. He always comes home with a gift for the kids anytime he takes them somewhere. His voice softens when he talks with the children—even if he is frustrated. He listens— really listens to hear and understand. He is a good guy."

I wrote a separate list for myself of things I would commit to in the next season. It wasn't a list to fix myself but to focus myself. I had repented, I had turned and faced God and his will for my life, but I needed tangible things to grasp. Otherwise I could drift and then turn around again.

Holy Spirit, help me, I prayed while writing. It seemed he helped me to write down the twelve actions I would pursue daily because God cares about our marriage more than we do. It's his deal, his design, his call on our life. The weight of healing rests on him, but we need to be willing to take the next right step with him. *I'm willing. Help me, Jesus.*

The twelve things I committed to pursuing daily were as follows:

1. Prayer, worship, and reading the Bible. I am doing it all—all the cheesy Christian stuff. I need to be filled with it.

2. Praying for our marriage. I will do this every time I am feeding the baby.

3. Doing the next right thing. Not giving up. Staring at the 0.6 percent of hope instead of the 99.4 percent of despair.

4. Saying, "*How* will God fix our marriage?" Not "*Will* God fix our marriage?"

5. Starting today, not letting myself say negative things about me, like, "I am a bad wife." Looking for the good in me. Shame has no hold on me.

6. Dwelling on the good of Matt. Writing it down. Saying it aloud to him and to others.

7. Hugging Matt at least once per day.

8. Reaching out to "my people" who know our situation—even when I don't feel like it.

9. Going for a run most days for my emotional, spiritual, and physical health.

10. Having fun with the kids—not looking to them to meet my needs but to bless them.

11. Not running from Matt emotionally. Working to stay present in his presence.

12. Giving to others even when I don't want to. In giving we receive.

As I woke up to how much damage the *what-if* questions and reasons to leave caused my marriage, I increasingly saw my own hypocrisy. I preached from the stage about how we need to love and serve all people *no matter what,* but I didn't love and care for my nuclear family. For my husband. I was acting like a hypocrite.

I decided that whether or not my sexual desires for Matt ever changed, I would show him love in the small ways I could.

Do what you are comfortable with and one half step more.

• • •

MATT

When Laurie confessed her fantasy about leaving our marriage, I knew I had to take action. She had taken a step toward me, and now it was my turn. I had been trying my best for years to maintain stoicism. Steadfastness. *Just don't do anything to make her run. Keep the peace.* But here she was, all in. Granted, it wasn't like a romantic movie where she flung herself wholly at me, but her foundation was grounded. She was choosing to surrender to God, and it both comforted and unnerved me.

Now what? The physical aspect—the part that pained me the most—was not changing. This was not the marriage I had been promised in junior high. Yes, she hugged me once in the morning, and she no longer wanted to run from any room I walked into, but there was still this whole sex thing—the idol that I didn't yet recognize as an idol.

Sure, I had stopped looking at porn, but that didn't mean sex wasn't still my highest priority in our marriage.

But before I could remove the idol, I needed some real strength to do so. Love holds the greatest power I know.

A key to unlocking this powerful love came from an unexpected place. We signed up for a five-day marriage intensive, three hours per day. That may sound like hell to some people, but I was looking forward to it. I wanted to learn something.

Laurie was the one who looked fearful. She had resolved to stay married but going to counseling as a person who experiences attraction toward the same gender is terrifying. Many therapists don't know how to walk with them. They either encourage the person to do whatever their hearts want ("Leave your spouse! Do what makes you happy!") or they shame them into some sort of pseudo-straightness ("Just have lots of sex with your spouse!"). Many counselors do not know how to walk well alongside same-sex attracted people who hold to a historical Christian view of marriage. Would this guy? We didn't know. I promised Laurie that if he started laying into her about her sexuality, I would stand up and walk out with her instantly. We were a team. No matter what.

We did not have to fear. For the first several days, most of our discussion centered around me. Some people are gifted with the ability of discerning how to unlock hearts, and this man had that gift. He could see that Laurie was not the only one shut down in our marriage—I was too.

Laurie locked away her heart because of a lack of desire and fear of me; I hid mine because I was afraid of her. Vulnerability is terrifying. It did not fit into my male paradigm of steadfastness and stoicism. Men are supposed to be strong, I believed. We are supposed to have the answers. When I saw Laurie in pain, my first reaction was not to rip open my own heart in shared vulnerability. Wouldn't that throw our marriage into turmoil? Didn't she need me to be strong?

But my need to be strong only pushed her away. My perceived strength only fueled her fear, shoving her further from me. I thought she needed a quiet, steadfast man who was impervious to pain, but that type of man scared her. *What is below the surface?* she wondered.

Laurie needed to know what lay beneath my surface. She needed my emotional vulnerability, which is terrifying when you know you could be rejected—when you have been rejected.

"Tell me about your birth," the therapist asked. We may not remember our first moments of existence, but many times our infant-life circumstances have a great effect on us.

My mom was a strong person who was born with several health complications. We still do not know the extent of them as she, like many of us, avoided sharing the pain of her inner world emotionally and physically. However, I do know that because of some of her birth defects, she was on a feeding tube until she was sixteen years old. Suffice to say, when she became pregnant with my brother several years later, the doctors were still worried about her health. When she got pregnant with me seven months after my brother was born, they were alarmed. They told my parents it would be wise to abort me. "At best he will be severely brain damaged," they said, "and at worst the pregnancy could kill both of you."

My parents were adamant: "No. He is our child no matter what."

I was born two months early in the mid-eighties. Neonatal technology was not as good back then as it is now, and both my mom and I stayed in the hospital for several months. When we were finally released, my mom was still in a fragile condition, but I had no brain or physical complications.

I heard this story growing up. My parents told me so that I would hear their fighting love for me, as well as God's provision. But I focused on the doctor's advice: kill him. *Doctors are smart,* I thought. *Doctors thought I shouldn't live. They didn't think I was worth saving. I must be worthless.*

The therapist stopped my story there. "Go back," he said. "Go back to your birth. Can you picture little Matt as a baby? Tiny Matt?"

He didn't use the same kinds of therapeutic techniques that came with my training, but I had been a Christian long enough to know that God can use anything. So I engaged.

"Yes, I can," I said, closing my eyes.

I could see little, four-pound me: tiny, helpless, alone, cold, and vulnerable in a small incubator, hooked to machines.

"How does that baby feel?" the counselor asked.

"Unwanted," I said, feeling weighed down by the statement.

"Now, ask Jesus, how does he feel about you?"

Suddenly, there were no tubes connected to me. There was no incubator. The warmth for the baby came from the strong hands of Jesus. He picked me up with a huge grin on his face. *He loves me.* It took my breath away and silent tears began to fall. Jesus said nothing. He just looked at tiny, helpless, needy, vulnerable me, and like a dad lion might do to a cub, he put his forehead to mine.

I see you. I affirm you. I want you.

I could not stop the tears. We spent a few minutes there as I wept, receiving the love of Jesus. I let my unlocked heart drink it in.

But the counselor and my heavenly Counselor weren't done with me.

"Then what happened?" he continued. "How did your heart get locked again?"

We moved ahead several years.

In addition to her health complications, my mom had an emotionally painful life. None of us truly know how deep her scars went because she refused to share the majority of her story with anyone.

As a child, my older brother, Josh, and I noticed that she withdrew from cultivating relationships, including with my dad. But she did not stop moving toward Josh and me. She adored us. She worked hard to make our favorite foods, to read us stories we loved, to watch SpongeBob and Star Wars with us, and when we were tasked with cutting the lawn, all ninety pounds of her cut "just the hard parts" for us. Our mother who had suffered so much, tried her best to make sure we suffered as little as possible.

But she had heart needs she couldn't silence. She longed to be seen, to be known, and to be loved. She did not always look to God to satisfy those needs. She looked to me and Josh. We were her false gods—her idols.

When we were preparing to go to college, her world came crashing down.

When idols are removed, we are shaken. When they are pulled from their sandy foundations, we often uncover the gangrenous wound we hoped to hide beneath the surface. Instead of brushing the soil aside, finding the pain, and healing it with the help of Holy Spirit-filled professionals and friends, we can grab the next idol to plug the stench. Many of us do this.

My mom did too. She chose alcohol to numb her pain. When that didn't work, she looked to suicide to numb it forever. One night, after a particularly painful evening of drinking, I looked into my mom's eyes and said, "Mom, when I go to college, you know I'll still be your son, right? I will always love you." I didn't know about her suicidal ideation. As a teen boy, I just thought she was having a bad day.

The next morning, she woke me up early with a big hug. "Matt," she said between dripping tears, "had you not said what you did last night, I wouldn't be here today." I shook myself awake, smiled, and told that story in youth group as a badge of honor of my heroic stoicism and care.

But that was not a role I was supposed to play: the hero. The perfect son whose empathy was reserved for everyone but himself.

I have needs too. Heart needs. Needs to be *loved*, to have *purpose*, and to be *desired*—not in a sexual way but as a person.

This need showed up as a child. The therapist led me to a memory of when I was about eight years old at the dinner table. My dad, mom, and brother often laughed together, having a good time. Many times I joined them, but sometimes I felt disconnected from the group, like I didn't belong. So I slipped away from the table to sit on the stairs—both halfway in the group and halfway out, wondering, *Will anyone find me here? Will anyone pursue me? I just want a friend. Someone who won't take from my emotional reserves but will fill them.*

There were times my mom or dad came. Other times, no one did.

In the office with this counselor and Laurie, I grieved the deep loneliness I had not known I felt. I yelled with anger from a place I hadn't known was angry. We all bury emotions, but they don't decay. They compound and calcify until someone comes along with right tool to set them free and get to the gangrenous wound below.

The therapist moved into that moment with tenderness. "Matt? Would you like a friend to sit with you on the stairs?"

"Yes," I said, wiping snot from my nose.

"Laurie?" he asked. "Could little, eight-year-old Laurie come and sit with you there?"

"Yes," I looked over at her and smiled, seeing matching tears fall from her eyes. Her heart wasn't as securely locked as I thought.

Laurie joined me on the stairs. "Hi," she said awkwardly, aware of her own emotional vulnerability in front another man, the male therapist. "Can I sit with you?" she asked me.

I nodded, laughing. "Yes."

She paused, focusing. "I'm sorry you're all alone here," she said in a voice that sounded young somehow. "I'm sorry you feel so alone. I won't leave you. I want to be your friend. Can I be with you here?"

I nodded again. *What is this I am feeling? Vulnerability and yet . . . freedom? With Laurie?*

We laughed together and simply sat. Physically in the counselor's office but emotionally as friends on the steps. Laurie reached for my real-life hand. *In public.* In recent months, Laurie had cried at the thought of doing something like that. She was so affected by the memory of her assault that to even envision walking around our neighborhood hand-in-hand with me brought her to tears. Now, here she was in front of another person, holding my hand for the briefest of moments.

When the exercise was done, we smiled genuinely from the soul at each other.

Gentle vulnerability with your spouse can be the key to unlocking each other's hearts.

Gentle vulnerability with the Father can be the key to unlocking your own.

Those hours opened and filled me with the type of empowering love that took me the next half step toward ridding myself of my idolatry of sex.

• • •

LAURIE

I journaled the next morning after our marriage intensive experience.

> I saw Matt's heart yesterday for the first time. The little girl inside of me reached out to the little boy inside of him. I saw him. And then the adult in me wanted to care for the

adult him. I *wanted* to see him. I *wanted* to show him I cared for him—as he was.

Can the little girl in me learn to love the little boy in Matt? Can that friendship grow and develop—in spite of orientation, in spite of sexuality, in spite of all of the ripping, horrific pain we have both endured? Can we learn to care for one another's hearts? Be safe places for one another?

I did not know, but I would take the next half step to see.

THREE

YESTERDAY

The great sinners and the great saints, in fact, are made of the very same "stuff"—a mad, burning, aching, wild desire for ecstasy. What's the difference? The great sinners head for the fast food while the great saints have discovered the living hope of the banquet.

And this, it seems, helps explain why great sinners are often the ones who become great saints. They may have been eating from the wrong menu, but at least they're in touch with their hunger, so when the banquet shows up, they're often the first to recognize that that's what they've been looking for all along.

CHRISTOPHER WEST

LAURIE

A few months after Juliette's birth and before my post–silent retreat repentance, we brought home a player piano.

We needed the music. Our marriage seemed to be holding on by nothing more than the rings on our fingers.

Like the von Trapps in *The Sound of Music*, my family of twelve siblings grew up very musical. We sang during chores, we harmonized on vacation drives in our fifteen-passenger van, we performed on church stages (accompanied by Baptist-church-approved dance moves), and we gathered around our baby grand piano while the second-oldest led us in our favorite worship songs.

When I was eleven, we moved into a new home that wasn't quite finished. The interior painters still had work to do, so they found ways to put down tarp, set up ladders, and roll out paint around our antics. They commented frequently about the noise—not the loud children but the singing. We thought it was normal to constantly fill our house with song, but having non-family members in our home for several months showed us we weren't as normal as we thought.

As the wall of fear and hostility grew between Matt and me, I remembered our childhood piano and singing. *Maybe it would help us if I brought outside piano music inside.* I couldn't always articulate my desire to fix our brokenness with words, but perhaps the music could say what I couldn't.

I found a free piano online and Matt, ever the servant, made a way to pick it up. With it came dozens of songs for us to pop in the spinning mechanism and sing together. In the first few days, Matt made us laugh by pretending to play the already-playing keys, and the old-timey melodies seemed to cut through the fog of hopelessness in our home.

One morning, he and our two-year old, Gwyn, jovially pumped the pedals to "Singin' in the Rain." I heard the laughter and came down to join them, bouncing Juliette on my hip. I smiled at both Matt and Gwyn, feeling my face crack slightly from freshly dried tears. Matt's back tightened, and he hesitated to make eye contact as he remembered the night before.

The assault memory was still vague, but my fight or flight response to Matt had kicked into high gear. We had enjoyed a good evening of connecting relationally, and Matt was hopeful for some sort of physical connection. Before the resurfacing of this memory, this would likely have not been a problem. But not anymore. All he wanted was to embrace me, but after thirty seconds, I felt like a bucket at the top of a cliff. The memory kicked me and I toppled into despair. Physically, I froze, turned away from Matt, and curled up into the fetal position.

Some people's response to trauma is fight. They hit back in rage at whoever is hurting them. For me, that would come later. At this time, my default was to flight. In the bed I shared with a person my subconscious perceived as evil and terrifying, I felt I had nowhere to run except deeper into myself. I curled up, envisioning ripping off my skin to feel *something* other than my shuddering anger toward Matt. I fought digging my nails into my arms, which seemed like it would siphon off some of the overwhelming pain I felt inside. I stared at the second-story windows. *Exit. Leave. Jump out.* Those three exits encircled my once beloved window seat. It was the reason I wanted to purchase this house. I daydreamed of evenings I would journal while looking over our backyard's sunset. I had done it several times since we moved in, but now my daydreams were infused with thoughts of death.

"Laurie?" Matt whispered, concerned. "Laurie? Where are you?" He hardly touched my back as he beckoned me from wherever my mind had gone. This was not the first or last time it would happen. Dozens of incidents would follow.

I could not talk. My jaw locked. *Say something. Talk to him.* There were parts of my heart that wanted to. I did love him. I did want to be close to him in many ways, but I literally couldn't. The verbal processing part of my brain, the Broca's area, had gone offline as my subconscious shifted from the present moment to the memory held in my body.[1]

After several minutes, I found a quiet voice and whispered, "I just want to go to sleep." I pulled my sleep mask over my eyes and drifted off into oblivion.

The next morning, I woke up, grabbed my coffee, and wrote to process what had happened. Tears came with the writing.

I don't want to feel more or feel again, God. Why did you let it happen? This whole stupid memory? I'm so angry at you. I'm so mad! All my anger . . . I can't take it out on you because you're not physically in front of me! I want to hurt someone or something. I want to hurt myself. Destroy myself. I don't want to feel. I want to run and scream and rip my skin off and do things that are dangerous and terrible to get away from the shame of it all.

Could you please kill me?

I see you holding me as I sob. You see what I want to do to myself, but you actually had it done to you. You let yourself be lacerated. Destroyed. Hurt. Pained. You were crushed for both my perpetrators and for me.

"Let me dole out the punishment," I hear you whisper. "You can never hate anyone enough—including yourself. Let me die for them and for you."

The rest of the family soon woke up, and after feeding Juliette, she and I went downstairs to join them at the piano. As they finished the final bars of "Singin' in the Rain," I scanned the titles of available songs. "Yesterday" by the Beetles stood out to me. As I handed it to Matt, he looked at me with a half smile. Matt popped it in and began slowly pushing the pedals to make the keys play the melancholy tune. The girls smiled and laughed as Mom and Dad began to sing—but I couldn't continue for more than a few lines before a sob caught in my throat. Our voices had mingled, doing what our hearts and physical selves could not.

Yesterday we could.

Last year we could.

In the beginning we could.

• • •

Matt had sat behind me in my favorite college class, Spiritual Formation. As an English major I didn't need it, but the wife of the couple who co-taught the course was my mentor and counselor, and I wanted to hear more from them. They were also two of the only people who knew about my double life: Christian campus leader by day secretly wrestling with her same-sex desires by night.

I shared with the wife, Cynthia, first. I could not look into her eyes as tears rolled down my cheeks. "I suck," I said over and over while sharing the story of the sexual relationship with my best friend. I felt so much shame over what I was doing and the only response that felt right was self-hatred.

The pervasive, shameful stickiness dripped off of me and onto the floor. What I was doing wasn't only wrong—who I was felt completely wrong. Perhaps if I hated myself enough, *somehow* that would rid me both of my shame and what I believed to be my shameful attractions.

But Cynthia didn't let me verbally eviscerate myself. She didn't even encourage looking down. Instead, she caught my eye, "Laurie, is that your name? 'I Suck'?" I didn't understand her question. *Of course, it is who I am.* I was irrevocably broken. A failure of a Christian. *That* was my identity.

In my mind, good Christians—especially good Christian girls— didn't wrestle with their sexuality (at least not in this form!). Good Christian girls wrestled with pride, anxiety, and perhaps desiring to have sex with their boyfriends. Many times, I wished I had their "normal" girl problems that could be shared during small group prayer requests.

Cynthia did not utter a word of shame toward me. She did not point out Bible passages that explore same-sex sexual relationships. Her eyes did not flicker with secret fear. She was peaceful and kind. When I mentioned suicidal ideation, she offered me her husband's card for counseling.

I met with Dave for months. Many times, I rolled out of bed with my girlfriend, drove to his office, and walked head-down into our appointment. He did not clobber me over the head with verses either. He never pointed me toward a need to be straight. He was patient and gentle, and anytime I asked for a bill, his eyes twinkled as he remarked, "Oh, you haven't gotten one yet? Hm. I'll have to look into it." He gave me thousands of dollars of therapy for free.

In that messy season, I edited our university newspaper and had my own review column titled "Get Out!" I encouraged fellow students to "get out" and off campus to try some of the restaurants and experiences I sampled with friends. However, I realized several months into the gig that I had a pattern in the people I took with me on my adventures: they were all women. *I should probably ask a guy to come with me,* I thought. *Who do I trust? Who isn't creepy?*

Matt Krieg. My first step of connection with him was to dub him "not creepy." At first blush, it is a comical start, but it meant there was something intangible about him that inexplicably, quietly drew my heart toward his own—not toward all men but toward him. And not in a primarily sexual way.

This is not an exclusive experience for marriages or relationships like ours. When Matt and I surveyed around one hundred straight and mixed-orientation couples, we found the top three initial attractors for *exclusively straight couples* were personality (73 percent), love for God (58 percent), and physical appearance (48 percent). In couples where one or more of the spouses' default sexual attractions are *not* toward the gender of their spouse, the top three initial attractors were love for God (73 percent), love for others (57 percent), and a shared, intangible heart connection (48 percent). Physical appearance showed up fourth (46 percent).[2]

The last one may seem strange to those who wonder about someone like me: "But you don't like guys. How does that physical appearance thing work *at all*?" I cannot speak for everyone who walks in similar shoes, but I could tell Matt was a good-looking guy just like I can tell you Hugh Jackman is a good-looking guy. My eyeballs can see, but my body doesn't automatically respond. I need things like hearing of his love for God, sitting with him as he loves others, and exploring more of that intangible heart connection to experience a physical draw toward him. The relational and emotional building blocks stand on each other to possibly lead toward a desire to connect physically. But again, we are not alone in this. Exclusively straight men and women say the same things: "I am not automatically attracted to him/her, but the emotional/spiritual can lead to a physical connection."

Following this intangible, heart-connected *something*, and compelled by the need to ask a man to join me, I messaged Matt to go on an adventure. I also invited another girl friend to come with us in case I had misjudged him. As we tried on spring fashion at a local thrift store and taste-tested a new pizza place, I discovered that Matt was not only nonthreatening, he was also funny. And deep. And he seemed interested in me—not because he wanted my body but because he seemed to like me as a person. This began to poke holes in my stereotypes of men and added strings of connection from my heart to his. A line from my counselor came to mind: "There are good men out there, Laurie. They just don't wear signs."

Maybe this is one of the good ones?

I invited Matt to join me on more outings with friends from church. Our friendship deepened as I noticed we communicated well and had a similar sense of humor. Matt learned that one of my love languages is breaking unimportant social "laws." We pretended to go furniture shopping at Art Van and drove sales attendants crazy when they realized we were only role playing as a couple searching for high-end goods. We rollerbladed past baffled grocery store managers and wrote Facebook messages to one another in Old English. Instead of laughing at my crazy ideas, he joined in. This man seemed different from other men.

But he still didn't know my deeper story—my hidden life. He did not know how many evenings I spent away from my group of friends, alone with the woman I called my best friend. She was, but she was also more than that. *If only we could stop crossing physical boundaries,* I thought. *Then it would be perfect! I wouldn't be sinning. We would just be best friends.* Then I could talk without shame to my executive pastor father, lead worship with the team without thinking of what I did the previous night, and hear sermons on idolatry without feeling the deep sting of conviction.

But that last one could never be true. I worshiped my best friend before our relationship turned physical. I made her my idol by focusing on her approval of me. Idolatry had begun before our relationship ever became sexual.

In fact, it did not begin with her at all.

Long before my same-sex relationship, I bowed down to the idols of achieving high grades, trying to be the perfect Christian role model, and earning affirmation from the right people. I beat myself up for less-than-perfect exam results. When I noticed a muddy area of my spiritual life, I polished it into a lesson I could share on a stage. If I felt someone didn't like me, I worked hard to sway their perception from an iffy frown to a smile.

My idols were church acceptable, but they were still idols. "The human mind is, so to speak, a perpetual forge of idols," John Calvin wrote.[3] Our hearts are idol factories. Because of the fall, we all have a natural default, predisposition, or orientation to meet the good needs of our hearts in ways that neither satisfy us nor glorify God. We were born that way.

From a young age, whenever I felt the draw toward women, I not only shoved it deeper into myself, I felt as if I had to cut it out of my thinking completely. "There is a war on marriage," I heard on Christian radio. "The 'homosexual agenda' is trying to destroy the family." I didn't want to destroy my family. I loved them. So whenever I felt attraction toward women, I fragmented myself to cope.

And cope I did—leaning instead on my performing, perfectionism, and people-pleasing idols. But the thing about idols is they cannot hold your weight. The year before I met Matt, I studied abroad at Oxford University. News flash: Oxford is academically rigorous. I could not get my usual perfect grades, which shattered my performance and perfectionism idols. Frantically, I looked toward winning the hearts of my classmates, but I could not speak the majority's intellectual language. A few

were kind enough to stalk Harry Potter filming locations with
me, but my idol demanded more than a handful of close friends.
It required a crowd, so my people-pleasing idol crumbled too.

I loved God as much as I knew how, but my identity did not
come from him. It came from doing well, from being perfect, and
from winning the most smiles from the right people. I was a
church-acceptable idol worshiper. When I met the woman who
would become my not-technically-girlfriend girlfriend, she
simply fell next in line at my heart's idol-making factory.

The difference was that she did not ask as much of me as my
performance, perfectionism, or people-pleasing idols. She saw
the real, gritty, imperfect me and shunned my former perfect,
sweating, smiling, treadmill lifestyle.

I felt free.

We could talk about our attractions with each other. We could
share the difficulty of resisting sexual temptation with each
other. We could talk about injustice in the church with
each other. We could talk about the secrecy church demanded
from us with each other.

Fighting both our default desires and the church brought
us closer.

I felt liberated . . . and yet in bondage (2 Peter 2:19).

Augustine said, "You have made us for yourself, O Lord, and
our heart is restless until it rests in you."[4] The answer to our
restless hearts can never be another person, activity, or job. It
can only be the holy, all sufficient, never empty Lord.

The closer my girlfriend and I became, the more we took our
eyes off of God and saw that our primary issue wasn't sexual—
we were two needy creatures looking to each other for fullness.

We were finite creatures and could not hope to fill the infinite,
aching holes in each other's hearts. "We feel lonely . . . and
thereby look—sometimes desperately—for someone who can
take away the pain: a husband, wife, friend," Henri Nouwen said.
"We are all too ready to conclude that someone or something
can finally take away our neediness. In this way we come to

expect too much from others. We become demanding, clingy, even violent."[5]

Our expectations made us jealous and controlling: our friendship became mutually addictive because the more we had of a finite person, the more we needed. We exchanged countless hours of conversation, set boundaries, and took many "breaks" to try to reset our relationship so that God was our primary priority. But it was too hard. *You fill me. You complete me.* If God had really been first in our lives, those sentences may have whispered to us, but we wouldn't have heeded them.

Jesus said we show our love for him through obedience to his commands (John 14:15).

But obedience is hard. It is costly. It requires loosening our embrace on our idols and replacing them with God—even if that leaves us feeling empty today. Even if it leads to suffering.

When we finally broke up, I suffered. Elisabeth Elliot, a woman familiar with suffering, defined it as "having what you don't want and wanting what you don't have."[6] I wanted my girlfriend to complete me rather than waiting on an intangible God to meet my needs in the new heavens and new earth (Revelation 21:3-4).

That seemed too far away and possibly like a lie—or at least an exaggeration. I couldn't imagine the fullness he promised later because of the pain I felt in the moment.

So even though I finally broke up with my girlfriend, I agonized over the decision. I wept over pictures of her, reread old text messages, and begged God to change his mind. I threw a tantrum at the feet of Jesus. But he didn't shame me for it. Even though he knew surrendering to his will was best for me, he did not shove that reality in my face. He sat with me in it.

Intangible as he is, I sensed his presence in the midst of suffering. I came to know his heart a little more. "Out of the deepest waters and the hottest fires have come the deepest things that I know about God," Elliot said.[7] "If we learn to know God in the midst of our pain, we come to know Him as one who is not a

High Priest who cannot be touched with the feeling of our infirmities. He is one who has been over every inch of the road."[8]

Jesus could shame us in our take-away-this-suffering tantrums, but he doesn't. Instead, he sits with us in them because he understands. He suffered too. He asked for his suffering to be removed too (Luke 22:42).

It was worth it for Jesus, and it was worth it for me. Not because God gave me a marriage to a man later but because any sacrifice that results in the world seeing us on our knees saying, "Not my will but yours," is worth it.

As I wrestled back and forth with making this permanent breakup decision with my girlfriend, Matt made his intentions clearer.

Nervous but curious about the invisible string connecting our hearts together, I asked Matt to pray about it for a month. I wanted to sort things out with my not-girlfriend-girlfriend and to pray for God to prepare Matt's heart to hear my real story.

God did. He'd begun years before Matt ever met me.

• • •

MATT

I grew up pretty classically homophobic. I didn't outright bully people who were gay, but I often treated "gay" as an interchangeable adjective for phrases like, "That's stupid," or "That's so dumb." Any person who overheard me while wrestling with attractions toward their same gender would have heard my words as a personal attack. Laurie would have heard my words as a personal attack.

It was culturally acceptable in my middle class, Christian circles to watch shows peppered with heterosexual sexual innuendo and respond with silence, or worse, to laugh along with the joke. But when a gay person showed up on the screen, we would ask with what we believed to be Christlike enthusiasm, "Why do they have to have a gay character?"

We were wrong. We were wrong to offer zero sensitivity to the real struggles of real people, and we were wrong not to realize we were ignoring the log in our own eyes (Matthew 7:4).

I was a hypocrite. I judged one type of sexual sinner while hiding my own sexual addiction.

In fifth grade, I walked into my friend's garage and looked up to see a swimsuit calendar. I both liked and disliked the feelings it stirred in me. I asked my friend's dad if I could take the calendar home to look at it more. He said I should ask my parents. They rightly said, "No," but without much explanation beyond, "We don't look at things like that."

That first accidental pornographic experience piqued my curiosity enough to search the internet. Years later, I was trapped in an addiction I felt I could not escape.

I am not alone in this. Sixty-five percent of young men, 33 percent of young women, 47 percent of adult men, and 12 percent of adult women (ages 25+) seek out porn regularly. It is also true that 57 percent of pastors and 64 percent of youth pastors currently struggle or have struggled with porn.[9]

The solution is not *only* to add porn blockers to our computers (I tried that) or to join a good accountability group (that helped temporarily). We have to understand why. Why is pornography appealing?

Ordained minister, licensed therapist, and author of *Unwanted: How Sexual Brokenness Reveals Our Way to Healing,* Jay Stringer conducted a survey of nearly four thousand people wrestling with unwanted sexual behavior. In his study he found countless connections between childhood wounding and general pornography use, as well as specific types of pornography engagement. For example, men who sought out aggressive pornography dealt with the greatest levels of shame, lacked significant purpose, and often had fathers who were overwhelmingly strict.[10]

"We need to learn to listen to our lust and see what it says about us," Stringer said.[11] As I listened to my own lust years into my marriage with Laurie, I heard that what I ran *toward* echoed what I ran *from*. I felt unwanted as a child, so I ran *toward* pornography in fantasies that were totally focused on myself. I was the hero. I was desirable.

I am not alone in this purpose-porn connection. Stringer's research found men are seven times more likely to escalate pornography use if they lack purpose in their lives.[12]

But the need to be desired or to have purpose is not a bad thing. Those are good needs, but going to pornography is a bad place for them to be met. Affirming my good needs—what Laurie and I call Core Needs—was critical in my healing journey, and it's something I teach all of my clients today.

Naming Core Needs is our imperfect attempt at putting language to what is inside of that God-shaped hole in our hearts. We believe God planted needs inside of us at creation to be met first and primarily by him, but he invites creation to support him in this need-meeting process for his glory.

Laurie and I had heard the concept of something similar in my counseling master's classes. My professors discussed Maslow's famous hierarchy of needs, which includes items like food, water, self-respect, and friendship. However, Maslow's not the only one to have discussed this idea of something good behind sinful desires—like the need for autonomy, identity, and competence.[13]
Here is our list:

Affirmed: overwhelmingly approved of
Desired: specially chosen; no pretense necessary
Included: wanted in this group, team, or partnership; feeling "I belong"
Loved: unconditionally accepted
Nurtured: cared for, held
Purposed: filled with a sense of profoundly mattering
Rested: re-centered and reset in mind, body, spirit; includes having fun
Delighted in: seen as unique and special

Protected: unafraid; trusting everything is under control

Noticed: seen inside and out

We formed this Core Needs list after my sexual brokenness came to the surface. We needed language to talk about my addiction because Laurie was so repulsed by it initially. "It fuels sex trafficking!" she said. "How could you?" I needed to be able to talk at a heart level. Laurie could hear and empathize there.

As we healed, we landed on ten Core Needs that seemed the most prevalent in our lives, the lives of my clients, and those Laurie discipled. They were also the needs we could find in the gospel narrative. To give an example of the gospel—Core Needs connection to my clients, I often say something like this: "God put a good need for *purpose* in us at creation, but the fall shifts this need for *purpose* into the demand to be *better than*. Jesus redeems this need by inviting us to confess ways we have turned away from him and modeling how we can experience true *purpose* by making disciples and serving others in our vocation and ministry life."

We believe everyone needs our ten Core Needs, but often times one or two stick out as our primary Core Needs. These are the ones that get depleted the fastest and can drive us toward unhealthy things.

But they are meant to drive us toward God. In the beginning, God created the world and called it good (Genesis 1:4, 10, 12, 18, 21, 25). He *affirmed* it. When he created people—the pinnacle of creation—he called us "very good" (v. 31). Very good—but still incomplete. Needy. God created us to belong or be *included* with each other in the body of Christ (2:18). Before the fall, we were also incomplete without a job to do. We needed *purpose*. So God gave what is called the "creation mandate" to cultivate the earth and subdue it.[14] These two needs, *inclusion* and *purpose*, are two of ten Core Needs—good things God placed in us to be met in him and supported by creation (people, our jobs, etc.).[15]

One of my primary Core Needs is the need to be desired. We define it as "specially chosen; no pretense necessary." It's visible at creation in how God desired us from before time began (Ephesians 1:4). Even reading the definition stings my eyes with tears. I am specially chosen. I don't have to pretend. I am wanted—as me.

Porn promised to meet this need: *You are chosen by us. You don't have to pretend here. We will desire you.* But it wasn't real. I felt desired for seconds. Minutes, maybe. But then I went back to my real life, lost my temper at my real family, felt shame and contempt at myself for what I was doing, and felt truly desired nowhere. So I went back to porn to feel better for seconds . . . minutes . . . and the cycle began again.

Another one of my primary Core Needs is the need to be protected. The definition we use is "unafraid; trusting everything is under control." We see this need for protection before the fall in the way Creator God placed boundaries in the Garden. "But the LORD God warned him, 'You may freely eat the fruit of every tree in the garden—except the tree of the knowledge of good and evil. If you eat its fruit, you are sure to die'" (Genesis 2:16-17). God laid out the rules not to outline what we are missing (*that* tree) but to circle where we can thrive and be truly safe (staying within the limits of the trees here).

But we ate from *that* tree. Therefore, every one of us inherits the curse. Because of the fall, our eyes and hearts naturally crave the fruit we cannot have and elevate it as ultimate.

Six years into our marriage, and five years after secretly restarting my pornography addiction, I looked to my job—a good gift—to be my god. But when we lean on the gift instead of the Giver, we find it cannot hold our weight. The moment I started to falter in my career, I could sense a whole-life imbalance. Instead of gripping Jesus' hand to steady me, I reached for more idols. More fruit. More gods instead of God. It wasn't always pornography, but it was usually a screen—football, a video game, hockey scores—often at the same time. I turned toward anything that would help me avoid the failures in my life.

But my idol worship began at a young age.

When I was three years old, my parents discovered I could kick a soccer ball equally well with both feet, so they enrolled me in the sport along with my older brother. Athletics became my safe place along with intelligence, as I found learning came naturally to me. There, I felt protected and desired. But instead of seeing sports and school as God-glorifying ways to emphasize his protection of and desire for me, I stared at them instead of seeing God through them. They became idols.

Encountering other people knocked these idols over. I did not always feel desired or safe with them. I often felt shaky and awkward when trying to form relationships because I did not know the next step.

In junior high, I sat on the school bus thinking of a silly song we had learned that day. I had a decent voice and enjoyed singing. I quietly sang to myself, feeling safe and happy being me. I had not yet learned it wasn't socially acceptable to do such a thing in middle school. A girl sitting in front of me with a mop of blonde hair took it upon herself to teach me. She turned around abruptly with a look of disgust on her face and asked, "What are you doing?" She covered her mouth without quieting her loud laughter. "Are you singing?" Others turned to look and snicker. My face reddened, and I swore at her. I acted like I didn't care, but I was covering my shame with contempt—contempt toward her and myself. That day, I swallowed my voice, buried it under anger, and vowed to never sing publicly alone again. I kept that vow until years into our marriage.

Many of us could recount story after story of situations where we shared our vulnerable voices only to be met by shame. But no matter the specific circumstance, every story leads to the same place: death. There are two types. The first is an unhelpful death where we try to kill the good needs in us, pretending we don't need to be desired, protected, or any of the other ten Core Needs.

"I am not needy," we say. "That's for weak people." But ignoring the needs of our hearts leads us down a path that ends in actual death. Our hearts need to be filled, and they will seek completion no matter what. They will turn to work, sex, food, marriage, friends, or any other outlet that promises satiation. We naturally go everywhere but God to find peace.[16]

The second type of death is helpful. Instead of killing our good needs, we put to death the idols that falsely promise to meet them. "That girl rejected me on the bus, but I need to be *delighted in* and *noticed*. I need to be *desired* and *affirmed*! Where can I get that need met?" We feel our needs, but we resist the pathways to temporary satisfaction and take them to the Father. Even if we do not *feel* filled by him immediately, we sit there in the uncomfortable emptiness and wait, building spiritual muscles, increasing endurance—knowing one day we will be completely filled forever.

I did not choose to surrender my idols or sit in my longing laser-focused on God. I chose the first death, almost literally.

I silenced my needs as much as I could, but they still demanded satisfaction. In junior high, when my friends called, I thought, *Maybe they desire to be with me!* But then they asked to talk to my older brother. *I am not wanted.* When I got good grades, I thought, *I am safe as long as I follow the rules.* But classes forced me to be around the other people in them, which made me feel shaky and unsafe.

This unpredictable, empty world overwhelmed me. In a matter of weeks, I quit soccer, hockey, and Boy Scouts—everything except school—and spent hours alone in my room, contemplating suicide. I knew my family loved me. But didn't they have to? I supposed God desired to be with me. But didn't he have to?

I decided to end it all one afternoon. *Will people even miss me? I'm done with this.*

But God wasn't done with me. As I looked at my belt in my hands and the rod in my closet, one of my favorite songs came on the radio: "Adam's Song" by Blink 182. The theme is loneliness and suicide, and the DJs often skipped the final verse. They didn't that day.

"Tomorrow holds such better days," one of the last lines echoed. Tomorrow.

I won't have a tomorrow if I do this. This is permanent. I realized as much as I felt deep despair, I wanted a tomorrow.

I put my plans on hold.

Within weeks, in God's sovereignty, he prompted members of my youth group to call and invite me to events. Not my brother— me. They unknowingly rescued me from the edge of a cliff and offered oxygen to my depleted lungs.

Their friendship didn't solve it all. I still viewed sex as an eventual idol to meet the needs of my soul in marriage. I tried to get my Core Need satisfaction from academics and sports. I didn't look beneath my addictions to the injured heart I considered worthless. But going through my own darkness had softened my heart toward others stumbling in it.

When I met Laurie, she didn't seem to have hidden areas of pain and depression. She was feisty, funny, and pushed me with her deep questions about life. One of our best conversations lasted hours on the roof of a house during a lightning storm. The flashes were far enough away that we were safe, but in the aura of God's fireworks, I shared for the first time about pressures to perform and tiptoed around my own wrestling with worthlessness. She alluded to understanding but did not share more of why.

I wanted to know but needed to wait until she was ready.

Months into our friendship, I recognized I liked her. Laurie could tell. "What is going on here?" she asked on the phone after a particularly sweet time hanging out. I had hugged her and could feel her stiffen. Had I gone too far? I was scared of losing her friendship.

"Well," I said slowly, "I like you. And . . . I'd like to date you." She was quiet. I figured this was where our friendship would end.

I had wrecked it with my failure to understand all of the relational rules.

"How about we pray about it for a month?" she suggested.

I was relieved but curious. Why a month? *Is this some sort of Christian school girl thing? Is she "dating Jesus" this month?*

Thankfully, Laurie didn't mention dating Jesus and our friendship continued normally for the next thirty days until one blustery spring morning. "I need to tell you something, and it might not be easy for you to hear," she began. We sat on top of a picnic table, the wind whipping through her long, blonde hair. She was impervious to the chill as she talked, walking me through her story, ending somewhere around, "I've been in this relationship with another girl, but I think I figured things out with her while we took this time to pray." (As I would learn later, they hadn't figured things out. They had tried—oh, they tried— to take their relationship back in time to friendship only. But it was too hard on them both. They wouldn't break up permanently until a couple of months after Laurie and I had started dating.)

"The attractions toward her are still there," Laurie continued, looking toward me but not into my eyes. "But . . . I am still interested in taking the next step with you. I don't know why. I just am." She dared to look into my face. "What do you think?" She cowered, seemingly waiting for my rejection.

How could I reject her? This was my friend. The one I roller-bladed with through grocery stores. The one who made me laugh and grimace while we annoyed salespeople. The one who made me think. She wasn't a stereotype. She was a fellow beloved and broken person . . . like me. She suffered like I did and wrestled with sexual brokenness in ways I understood. She was funny, deep, and scrappy, and none of that changed when she shared her story.

"I don't see you any differently," I said. And I meant it.

"You don't?" She seemed shocked.

"How could I?"

She looked at the backs of her hands, blinking back tears.

"I would still like to pursue something with you . . . if you want to," I said tentatively.

"I do." She laughed, relieved. "But I don't know what it will look like!"

"Me either." I shook my head. If people in general made me feel out of control, this relationship would make me feel doubly out of control. And yet strangely safe because neither of us knew what we were doing. Someone else had to run the relationship for us.

"Can our dating just be like what we have been doing? Being silly and also deep and friendship that leads . . . I don't even know," she trailed off.

"Yeah," I said. "Silly, deep, friendship dating sounds good to me." I smiled, feeling like an awkward middle schooler again. But this time, I wasn't singing alone.

• • •

LAURIE

Yesterday . . .

The song ended, but the tears didn't stop. *Do I want to go back to yesterday?* We were so naive when we said yes to dating. We were so naive when we promised a lifetime of covenantal love. *Would I make the same choices if I could go back?*

I chuckled, wiping the tears away as I remembered those early days of ultimate frisbee and rollerblading and rooftop lightning storm conversations. "What?" he asked, hopeful at my laugh.

"We had some good times in the beginning." We weren't pretending then. Our love, friendship, different-sort-of dating, and then marriage wasn't false. I just didn't know how hard it would be. I didn't know it would feel so impossible.

He didn't either.

Our eyes connected. "I still love you," I said.

He sighed, his hands falling from the piano keys. "I know. I love you too."

My glance fell to the ground. It was dangerous to feel connected. It led to his desire to show me physically. My neck muscles tensed. I could not do that. Not yet. Maybe not ever again.

God, help me, I said quietly, walking with Juliette back up the stairs. *I don't understand why it has to be male and female in marriage. I don't understand why sex has to be a part of this at all. Please, teach me the good of sex in male-female marriage.*

He would, while simultaneously teaching Matt it is not the ultimate good.

FOUR

THE PURPOSE

It's tough being a Christian in today's world. It's tough being a husband or a wife; it's tough making family life work. But that is because it is a sign and a symbol of the most extraordinary divine plan, the plan which cost God himself the death of his own beloved son.

N. T. WRIGHT

LAURIE

About a month into dating Matt, I told him I never wanted to get married. "It sounds terrible," I said honestly.

As I listened to the complaints and watched the silent bristling between married people around me, it seemed like there was a big bait and switch when it came to marriage. Marriage veterans clapped for dating couples in front of them, then elbowed and nodded about how hard it was behind their backs.

In the 1990s, people were beginning to question the age-old promise that if you got married, all of your dreams would come true. Christians saw the alarming divorce rate and scrambled to respond. Their response, however, seemed to be, "Let's get real about how tumultuous it is." This was helpful for those walking through the challenges of marriage, but those of us who were unmarried and listening to the conversation thought, *But why do it at all? If marriage equals pain, why get married?*

Maybe it is for the relational closeness, I considered. *You get a permanent best friend.* But marriage doesn't solve the loneliness problem. According to a recent study on loneliness by UCLA, about one in three married people over the age of forty-five feel lonely.[1] Additionally, as I listened to how couples spoke about their marriages, I heard a desire for *more* loneliness (or at least alone time) because men and women were so different.

"Ugh. Men burp, fart, are stupid, lazy, cannot relate emotionally, and all they want is sex!" some women said.

"Ugh. Women are nagging, annoying, controlling, whiny, and they don't stop talking!" some men said.

Then why marry someone of the opposite sex? I wondered. Men seem to like men better, and women seem to like women better.

Maybe it is for sex, I considered. Marriage made sex legal for Christians. But as I listened to the conversation around sex through sermons and radio, I heard more complaints and eye rolls. And the worst, in my opinion, was women just needed to "do it more."

"Women, we need to serve our husbands. Make sure he's shopping in your store, or he'll go somewhere else," women said.

"Men, we need sex. Serve your wife in the kitchen, and you will get some," men said.

But the weight of having sex seemed to be on the women who gave to the men. If the wife mentioned her own sexual needs, they were unquestionably secondary to her husband's. This led to more scoffing and eye rolling of the women toward "lazy and stupid" men.

Then why marry someone of the opposite sex? I wondered.

And yet here I was, dating a guy. *But we're different from other couples,* I thought. *We won't be like those who simply tolerate or secretly resent each other. Our foundation is friendship. It's something bigger than hormones: it's an intangible heart connection.*

But that was not enough to keep us from becoming exactly like the couples I judged.

Eight years into our marriage, we were still friends . . . but I didn't have to be married to Matt to be his friend. We communicated well, but we were both generally good communicators. We could have fun together, but we could have fun with many people. We loved Jesus, but our relationship with him seemed individual to each of us. We worked well together—our house stayed clean, the bills were paid, and our kids were cared for—but was that fruit of a solid, rich, deep marriage?

One therapist described our relationship as "cordial," and he was right. We worked well together. After recommitting to Matt on my silent retreat, I had lost my secret resentment toward him, but we had still become like the couples I judged before getting married. That intangible heart connection that drew me into dating and marriage was now gone. We just . . . lived. The only difference for us was that sex was off the table. (And there are more married couples—including straight ones—than we realize who are just like us in this area.[2])

But does sex have to be back on the table? I wondered. *Is sex a need?*

It seemed like it was the key ingredient to every romantic relationship. What was the climax of every romantic comedy movie? A fade-to-black sex scene. Why were men kind and serving to their wives? So they could have sex after the kids went to bed. What did pastors say about sex in marriage sermons growing up? "It is the barometer of a good marriage."

Sex seemed like the goal of marriage—not hearts connecting, not linking arms and running toward Jesus. This frustrated me as someone who was still working through trauma and who did not automatically feel attracted to her husband. If sex was the barometer of a healthy marriage, then ours was about to keel over and die.

But sex is not a need in general, I thought. The Christian faith teaches that sex is reserved for marriage and that single people are to remain celibate.[3] Do single people have less-than lives because they don't have sex? If that's the case, then Jesus himself must have had a less-than life. The same goes for the apostle Paul and everyone else who has ever said God has called them to singleness. *But that can't be true,* I thought, *because Paul lifts up singleness as superior in many ways to marriage.*

> I say to those who aren't married and to widows—it's better to stay unmarried, just as I am. . . . I want you to be free from the concerns of this life. An unmarried man can spend his time doing the Lord's work and thinking how to please him. But a married man has to think about his earthly responsibilities and how to please his wife. His interests are divided. (1 Corinthians 7:8, 32-34)

If singleness is at least equally as good as marriage, and sex is reserved for marriage, is sex only a need in marriage? And if so, why?

I could not consider this question theologically or relationally without also working on it psychologically. Matt no longer pushed me to see a therapist, but I chose to go on my own. My therapist helped me put words to the panicked fight or flight I felt. "That's your little girl inside who got stuck at the age you were traumatized. She can't put to words what she feels when she is triggered, and so she hides or tries to fight back." I was learning to be kind to her—to me. When I was triggered, I slowly trained myself to say, "You are an adult. You are safe. You don't have to be afraid." It did not remove the memory, and it did not fix me, but it gradually taught me how to cope.

As I worked on caring for the little girl inside of my heart, my adult brain had some questions.

"Laurie," Matt said gently one evening after our small group, "it's a bit disturbing that you're running a ministry around sexuality and yet you do not believe in its goodness."

We were processing our separate conversations with the men and women at our group, and he told me how he shared with the men how much he was growing when it came to physical intimacy. "Even though it's been off the table in our marriage for a year, I have still been worshiping it," he repeated to me. "I still saw it as an answer to my problem. God has been molding my heart. He is showing me what I truly need is him. And as I get closer to him, I want a heart connection with you instead of primarily a physical one. Sex is not a need. God is."

"But you still want it?" I said, cold to his kind words. I may have lost the general resentment toward Matt, but anytime sex was brought up, my heart refroze. "You still want to have sex with me?"

"Yes," he said gently, knowing this was a tough conversation for me. "But, Laurie, you act like that is a bad thing."

I swallowed a retort. How dare he shame me like that? But as I sat with his statement, I could see that he wasn't wrong and he wasn't shaming me. My job and calling were to educate the church on how to walk with people wrestling through issues related to sexuality. I could talk all day about how it is not ultimate and how we are all broken sexually, but I could not give a talk on why God designed sex as a good thing because I did not believe it.

Matt was right. "You're not wrong," I admitted halfheartedly. I saw only brokenness when it came to sexuality. People sexually assaulted kids. Men and women were addicted to porn. Men and women used sex as a power play in their marriages.[4] One person seemingly always felt dissatisfied. I could talk to any adult person for one minute and hear at least one story of sexual brokenness in their life.

"I think God made humans broken when he made us sexual," I continued. "Look at the world! Look at church world, pastor world, and abuse . . . pornography! God made a bad thing."

"Or did I make a good thing and the enemy turned it upside down?" The Holy Spirit spoke to me as clearly as if Matt responded.

Matt was quiet. "I don't feel like I can or should say anything. You are going to have to hear from God on that."

I already had.

Fine, God, show me. Teach me how it is good.

I began my quest by asking people. I peppered trusted, older couples with questions. I wanted to hear stories from both the husband and wife about how sex is more than a physical act, one that gives life to both of them. Men could more easily say, "It's good," but the wives' eyes often flashed with the unsaid words, "I tolerate this."

I asked our mentor and friend if sex was good for him and his wife. "It seems like all men want to do is get off, and the women want their husbands to get off of them."

He laughed. "If you would ask my wife right now, she would tell you it is rich. Bone-deep rich—even better as the years go on." My eyes narrowed, searching his for a trace of a lie, but I could tell he was telling the truth.

I needed something greater than his word. I needed a foundation more than even bone-deep connection. If I heard God right in what he said to me—that it was good but the enemy had used it for evil—I needed his perspective on the purpose of sex.

To do that, I needed to back my vision up to understand the purpose of marriage. To do that, I needed to understand the purpose of life.

• • •

Let's go back to it. The purpose of life is to serve as image bearers of a holy God, pointing to him in everything we do and pointing to Jesus as our rescuer.

This is the goal for *all people*, married and single alike: Love God. Make disciples.

Okay, but what about married people? If our individual purpose is to glorify God and make disciples, then why get married? Couldn't we live out our purpose as single people? We've already established marriage is hard, it doesn't answer the loneliness problem, and sex doesn't solve our issues . . . so what is the point?

To discover this answer, I pored over the Bible while picking up marriage book after marriage book. Most were written by men, which was a challenge to my skeptical, injured soul. Many relied on joking about the differences between men and women to gain rapport with their audience, which only enticed the default response of my sin nature: "Well, then I will marry someone of the same sex!" But one book resonated because of its focus on God rather than the married couple: Francis and Lisa Chan's *You and Me Forever*.

Within its pages, Francis and Lisa explore the connection between the purpose of life and the purpose of married life. It's about God. It's about his will. His mission. They never jokily disrespected one another to connect with their readers. Rather, they demonstrated reverence for God, genuine mutual love, and a passion to make disciples together. There was less of a focus on the problems of wedded bliss than on the joy of reflecting the king.

Our marriage problems are not really marriage problems. They are heart problems. They are God problems. Our lack of intimacy with God creates a void that we try to fill with frail substitutes, like wealth, pleasure, fame, respect, people—or marriage. But we can't cure our narcissism by trying to ignore ourselves. The solution is to gaze upon God. When we do, everything else fades into its proper place.[5]

I could hear this holy awe, this universal call to oneness with each other and the king. As I read their words and wrestled through the Word, I began to more clearly see the purpose of marriage: to serve as a visible representation to a broken world that God loves them and wants to be one with them.

Ephesians 5 tells us as much: "For this reason a man will leave his father and mother and be united to his wife, and the two will become one flesh. This is a profound mystery—but I am talking about Christ and the church" (vv. 31-32 NIV).

People have taken these verses to answer the question, "Why do people fall in love?" With sparkling eyes and a big sigh, they say, "It's a great mystery."

No! Falling in love is not a part of these verses. That's not the mystery. "The mystery is not marriage between a man and a woman, but the marriage between Christ and the church," Chan wrote. "It is a miracle that human beings can be united with God!"[6]

Most sermons I've heard on oneness were at weddings, but in their description of oneness the metaphor seemed inverted. Officiants alluded to the oneness-with-God mystery but only as a way of emphasizing how to connect as husband and wife—not to underscore the outrageous truth that humans made from dust are united with the Creator of the cosmos. The more I studied the metaphor of oneness, the more I grew convinced that every marriage sermon should be followed by a face-down worship session because the wedding whispers to our souls of what is to come (Revelation 21:2-3).

God will marry us. God will complete us. This is not a Hallmark movie—it is our saving grace.

Marriage only makes sense if it tells a bigger story, especially to someone like me who lacks a natural attraction to the opposite sex but is called to marriage. Our gender differences highlight that as different as men and women may be, we are nowhere near as different as God is from us. Yet God calls married people to be one (Matthew 19:6).

As I studied this notion of two different things becoming one, I began to notice the marriage metaphor all over the Bible.

In Genesis 1 and 2, God creates complementary opposites: night and day, land and sea, animals of the sky and the ocean, and in the end, man and woman.

> Then the LORD God said, "It is not good for the man to be alone. I will make a helper who is just right for him." . . . Then the LORD God made a woman from the rib, and he brought her to the man. . . .
>
> At last!" the man exclaimed.
> "This one is bone from my bone, and flesh from my flesh! She will be called 'woman,' because she was taken from 'man.'"

This explains why a man leaves his father and mother and
is joined to his wife, and the two are united into one.
(Genesis 2:18, 22-24)

The climax of all of creation is a wedding—two united into
one. But the marriage language continues. In the Old Testament,
when God's people do not obey, the Lord does not say, "You broke
the rule, and you are disciplined." Instead, he uses language like,
"You cheated on me!"

Then the LORD said to me, "Go and love your wife again,
even though she commits adultery with another lover. This
will illustrate that the LORD still loves Israel, even though
the people have turned to other gods and love to worship
them." (Hosea 3:1)

Long ago I broke the yoke that oppressed you and tore
away the chains of your slavery, but still you said, "I will not
serve you." On every hill and under every green tree, you
have prostituted yourselves by bowing down to idols.
(Jeremiah 2:20)

But the ever-faithful husband, God, continues to woo us, his
people, his bride.

Never again will you be called "The Forsaken City" or "The
Desolate Land." Your new name will be "The City of God's
Delight" and "The Bride of God," for the LORD delights in you
and will claim you as his bride. Your children will commit
themselves to you, O Jerusalem, just as a young man
commits himself to his bride. Then God will rejoice over
you as a bridegroom rejoices over his bride. (Isaiah 62:4-5)

Jesus continues the marriage language when he's asked why
his disciples do not fast like other disciples by responding, "Do
wedding guests fast while celebrating with the groom? Of course
not. But someday the groom will be taken away from them, and
then they will fast" (Luke 5:34-35). Christ is the groom, his disciples the attendants.

Then, the end of the Bible foreshadows our future. John paints a picture from his vision of what we will all see one day.

> "Let us be glad and rejoice, and let us give honor to him. For the time has come for the wedding feast of the Lamb, and his bride has prepared herself. She has been given the finest of pure white linen to wear." For the fine linen represents the good deeds of God's holy people. And the angel said to me, "Write this: Blessed are those who are invited to the wedding feast of the Lamb." (Revelation 19:7-9)

The greatest story starts with a wedding and ends with a wedding. "If a book begins with something and ends with the same thing, the author is telling you, 'That's what the book is all about,'" says Tim Keller. "The Bible is saying to you, in a marriage between a husband and a wife, you have a clue to the meaning of the universe and of history."[7]

And what is that clue to the meaning of the universe? God so loves the world that he gave up everything to be one with us.

Our marriages—through our differences—need to tell that story.

But how? How do we do that in real life, especially when it comes to sex?

• • •

MATT

As I signaled to merge into the left lane of the expressway toward home, Laurie and I processed our time with our small group. We loved those people deeply. Laurie had been friends with the wives of two of the couples for a while, and when they both separately expressed a desire to gather more often than Sunday mornings, we formed a grittily honest group.

Each couple took turns leading, and that night the lead pair had recommended we split up as men and women to share life updates and to pray over each other. I was grateful. I needed a safe space to open up. The other two guys were some of the only people who really knew what was going on with our marriage. They knew how I struggled to stay present and kind in the middle of Laurie's silent anger waves, they knew how long it had been since we were close physically, and they knew I was committed to staying no matter what.

That night, they learned how to come alongside me in a new commitment.

I had begun fasting from my desire for sex. Every time I have shared that sentence with others, their faces go blank. "What does that mean?" they ask.

The idea came to me after one of our pastors preached a sermon on fasting. "Fasting is the physical exclamation point at the end of this sentence: 'This much, oh, God, I long for you!'"[8] When we fast from a good thing, like food, we are supposed to use those physical hunger pangs to say to God, "This much, oh, God, I long for you."

Did I long for God? Could I long for him in the midst of my desire? When Laurie turned away from me again, put her sleep mask over her eyes again, and acted in a way that again felt like a rejection of my person, could I take that good, physical, emotional, spiritual longing for sex to God? *This much, oh, God, I long for you.*

I didn't know if I could, but I wanted to try.

"Every night, when Laurie turns away from me," I shared with the guys, "my mind shifts from sadness, to anger, to looking at God. 'God! Please help Laurie. Please heal this physical aspect in our marriage.'" Both Ryan and Caleb nodded. "But my prayers reflect what I worship: I want sex with my wife more than I want God in my life."

It felt holy to pray for what we did not have. But even though I talked to God first about what I did not have, my conversation with him revealed that God was not first in my life. *God, give me . . . God, I want . . . God, fix her so that . . .*

I did not love God with all of my heart, soul, and mind (Matthew 22:36-39). It wasn't even that I loved myself more than

I loved God because a defining quality of love, according to Scripture, is that "it is not self-seeking" (1 Corinthians 13:5 NIV). I was self-seeking. I was me-centered, not God-centered.

I certainly was not Laurie-centered. Even though I prayed for Laurie, my reasoning was all about me! *I* wanted comfort. *I* wanted to feel connected to her in every way. I did not truly care for her and what she needed in this season.

If I truly loved Laurie like Jesus loved me, I would give up my life—my wants—so that she could know how much God loves her (Ephesians 5:25). Laurie could only experience a filling of God's love for her in her deepest places of longing if her reason for pursuing healing was not for me but for her. She had to want healing because *she wanted healing*. I needed to give her space to be her own person, no matter the results. She did not need me tapping my toe until she healed from her trauma.

She may never get through this, I learned to pray. *But Father, with your empowering, I will be more than okay. You satisfy me, God.* The prayer was less of a declaration and more of a desperate call for it to be true. *I want to want you more than anything else.*

When I told Laurie about my fasting, she looked at me like I had just grown a third eyeball. "Okay . . ." She didn't understand. I tried to explain without triggering in her a cloud of shame and self-hatred. Sometimes, when we talked about the brokenness in our relationship, she turned the knife on herself and said, "If only I were 'fixed,' your life would be better."

Before the fast, it was always a challenge to explain that although I desired to physically connect with her, I still loved and cherished her deeply. I hoped that giving up the desire for sex would demonstrate both physically and subconsciously that I wanted her to heal for her. I did not need results. All I cared about was that she could more fully experience God's love. Period.

I thought giving up pornography and turning to my wife was enough. No. To mimic Jesus, I needed to give up everything and love no matter what. That was being like Jesus.

You must have the same attitude that Christ Jesus had. Though he was God, he did not think of equality with God as something to cling to. Instead, he gave up his divine privileges; he took the humble position of a slave and was born as a human being. When he appeared in human form, he humbled himself in obedience to God and died a criminal's death on a cross. (Philippians 2:5-8)

As we continued driving home, I offered some of what I had shared with the guys. "God has been working on my heart. He is showing me what I truly need is him. And as I get closer to him, I want a heart connection with you before a physical one. Sex is not a need. God is."

"But you still want it?" she asked sharply. "You still want to have sex with me?"

"Yes," I said as tenderly as I could. "But, Laurie, you act like that's a bad thing." *Was that okay to say?* Because of the Holy Spirit's conviction of my prayer life, I was now focused on my heart—but could God release me to exhort her too? I was grateful she dove in instead of cowering at my question.

In the following months, I watched her grill our mentor, our therapist, and other friends over the actual gifts of sex in their marriages. I saw her pick up book after book on marriage and bring the ideas she found to me. She wanted to see if and how these ideas applied to real life.

One conversation led to an epiphany for us both.

"Many of these books and podcasts I listen to explore how emotional connection leads women to connect to men physically," Laurie said. "Likewise, men open up to women emotionally through the gateway of the physical." Her jaw tightened, perhaps feeling threatened by this idea. "But the stereotypically emotional ones—us women—seem to come off as inferior in these conversations. We are the poor, helpless, emotional women, and you are the strong men who can legitimately overpower us." I got what she was trying to say: the fact that men are physically stronger and can (and have and do) overpower women to get what they want isn't right.

"Yes," I agreed, "we are often stronger physically." I paused, listening to what was going on in my body in that moment. I felt afraid. Why? I was not threatened physically. Why did I feel threatened? Why did I feel weak? "But you are stronger emotionally."

Her eyebrows went up. "I am." And women often are. Laurie's dad often jokes that she can feel the molecules move in the air with her emotional sensitivity. Not every woman is like this, but often women are more adept at engaging matters of emotions than men. (And I say this as a licensed therapist whose job is to engage emotions! I am good at it but not as naturally as many women.)

"We both have strengths that we need to steward to draw the other person out as opposed to dominating them," I said.

"You're right." I could see her wheels spinning. "I am often angry that it seems like men want an orgasm more than anything else, but we women stereotypically want an emotional . . . orgasm more than anything else." She laughed. "We want to reach a point in a conversation where we say, 'Yes! We connected.' We want an emogasm."

I chuckled.

"We do, though!" she continued. "You joke that I wear a scuba suit when it comes to relationships while many in the world wear snorkels." I did say this quite often. Laurie is able to explore people's emotional pain at a deep-sea level. Not everyone can or wants to do this—they prefer surface-level conversations. "But I cannot demand a deep emotional connection with you, just like you cannot demand a physical connection with me. If we want to love and care for each other well, to submit to each other," she continued, "we need to steward where we are powerful to draw the other out, as well as engage the other in their strengths to demonstrate love."

She was right. If I want to love Laurie as I love myself, then I will engage her like I want to be engaged. I would like her to move toward me physically, so I will move toward her where she is strong—emotionally. This means I will start deep conversations. I will ask questions to explore her inner world. I will get to know her heart.

To engage someone where they are strong speaks volumes to the one with the strength. To pursue Laurie emotionally, I am essentially saying to her, "I love you. This is hard for me, but you are worth it." That act builds intimacy because I have to trust that she will steward her emotional strength well.

Additionally, my vulnerability in submitting to her strength builds more connection between us. "We cultivate love when we allow our most vulnerable and powerful selves to be deeply seen and known," Brené Brown said.[9] Laurie sees and knows me deeply when I enter her place of strength. She does not make fun of my emotional conversation attempts. She does not abrasively call me out if I make a mistake. She affirms and welcomes me there. When this happens, not only do I feel loved, but she feels loved as I pursue her heart emotionally. I am speaking her heart language, and she is filled by it.

But unlike the stereotypes, I do not do this so that I can get some. That would not be love—that would be the epitome of self-centeredness.

Furthermore, if our marriage is a metaphor of Christ's love for the church, how does Jesus pursue us? He does not pursue our hearts so that we will obey—move to a foreign country to be a missionary, tithe more, feed the homeless, and so on. He pursues our hearts because that is who he is. He is love (1 John 4:8).

Our physical response to his pursuit of our hearts should become our natural response to his loving commands (John 14:15).

If I am to truly embody the reality of Christ's marriage to the church, I will pursue Laurie's heart for no other reason than the desire to love her well. And by me loving her unconditionally, the world will see how unconditionally Jesus loves them.

If Laurie wants to love me well, she will work to engage me where I am stronger and feel the most loved. I know she is physically weaker than I am, but the physical area of connection is also more challenging for her. Because of this, I treasure any approach toward me. A side hug. Grabbing my hand. A quick back rub. I see it and smile. It says to me, *I see you. This is hard for me, but I love you enough to try to engage you here.* The vulnerability connects us.

But she does not engage me physically in order to connect emotionally. She does not use physical connection as a currency to purchase what she wants. She engages me physically—in ways that she can—because she wants to show me God's love for me.

When we, the church, choose to give of our time, money, or energy—even if we are not one hundred percent excited about it—we are to give because we are motived by love. Often, our emotions—the joy of physically giving to God by giving to others—follows our obedience.

Pause. We need to note that this is an incredibly precarious and potentially treacherous path to walk when we put the metaphor of marriage next to relating to God physically through giving to others. Some might argue that just as God asks us to give to him physically by giving to others, so women ought give themselves physically to their husbands whenever they ask.

Yikes. How often has that kind of parallel been used to abuse a spouse? "You will give to me because I am the man!" husbands can say. I have heard recommendations for wives to simply have sex with their husbands *no matter what* because then the loving emotions will follow. Emotions follow obedience, they say. For women who have experienced zero trauma, zero spiritual abuse in this area, and who wrestle zero percent with same-sex attractions, this *may* be a helpful offering. But for women like Laurie who have been hurt by men, are attracted to women, and grind their teeth because they feel assaulted by such teachings—we need to push pause.

First Thessalonians 5:14 says, "Brothers and sisters, we urge you to warn those who are lazy. Encourage those who are timid.

Take tender care of those who are weak. Be patient with everyone." Laurie is anything but a weak woman. Talk to her for four seconds and you will hear the fire in her soul and strength from Jesus. But she will admit weakness in the area of physical touch—not just with me but with everyone. Am I to warn her? Even gently encourage her toward physical oneness in this season? No. I can express desire, but as the husband—charged by the Holy Spirit to love my wife as Christ loved the church, to give up my wants and my life for her—I am to take tender care of her.

After we danced around the strengths and weaknesses conversation for a while, Laurie looked at me with less skepticism or fear than I had seen in a long time. "I have strength," she said with finality. "I have power in this relationship," she paused, looking at me hesitantly. "And I have responsibility to care for your heart too."

I smiled while keeping my heart as open as I could. It hurt to continually be rejected, but I would do it. With the same power that raised our rejected Savior from the dead, I could do it.

FIVE

ONENESS, EVEN WHEN WE MARRY THE WRONG PERSON

When the glamour wears off, or merely works a bit thin, they think they have made a mistake, and that the real soul-mate is still to find. . . . Hence divorce, to provide the "if only." And of course they are as a rule quite right: they did make a mistake. Only a very wise man at the end of his life could make a sound judgement concerning whom, amongst the total possible chances, he ought most profitably to have married! Nearly all marriages, even happy ones, are mistakes: in the sense that almost certainly (in a more perfect world, or even with a little more care in this very imperfect one) both partners might have found more suitable mates. But the "real soul-mate" is the one you are actually married to.

J. R. R. TOLKIEN

LAURIE

When it comes to those of us who identify as not-straight and are married to someone of the opposite gender, the world would say that we married the wrong person. After all, we married the wrong gender. *You have an impossible marriage.*

But everyone marries the wrong person—no matter their sexual orientation. We all have an impossible marriage.

Duke University ethics professor Stanley Hauerwas said this:

We always marry the wrong person. We never know whom we marry; we just think we do. Or even if we first marry the right person, just give it a while and he or she will change. For marriage, being [the enormous thing it is] means we are not the same person after we have entered it. The primary problem is . . . learning how to love and care for the stranger to whom you find yourself married.[1]

Are you the same person you were five years ago? Ten? Twenty-five? No. We change. Romantic comedies that show couples sadly saying, "You are not the same person that I married years ago," as the logical reason to leave one another are out of line. Of course we aren't the same people we married years ago—that's the point of a healthy marriage! We are to help each other look more like our eternal selves. Tim Keller puts it this way:

> Within this Christian vision of marriage, here's what it means to fall in love. It is to look at another person and get a glimpse of what God is creating, and to say, "I see who God is making you, and it excites me! I want to be part of that. I want to partner with you and God in the journey you are taking to his throne. And when we get there, I will look at your magnificence and say, 'I always knew you could be like this. I got glimpses of it on earth, but now look at you!'"[2]

At the altar, instead of committing to this sanctification journey like our vows promise, we often silently say, "I like the way you make me feel. Keep doing that." Then, when we run into the reality that the other person has thoughts, feelings, wants, and a sin nature that bumps into that cozy feeling, we become shocked and angry.

This is where some marriage books step onto the scene. They seek to answer the shocked and angry predicament by offering tips on how to be more unified. In my marriage to Matt, I recognized this male/female difference dynamic, but when I tried reading marriage books, most of them didn't capture the extra level of difference we experience. Yes, he is male and I am female, but he had no major trauma growing up. I did. He was attracted to women and, well, so was I, but *that* seemed vastly different from straight-only marriages!

I was tired of reading these books and seeing only footnotes when it came to our marriage type. "For some reason, some women and men cannot connect because of trauma or other issues," they said. When I looked up the footnote next to their phrase "other issues," I might see something like, "If you experience attractions to the same gender, see a counselor. If you've experienced trauma, read a trauma book. If you've experienced both? Read . . . something other than this marriage book for regular people. You are weird." Okay, none of them really said all of that, but it felt that way.

I was tired of our level of differentiation going unacknowledged, but I was also tired of being relegated to another book, to a counselor, and to a "see other issues" footnote. If 20 percent of millennials identify as LGBT+ right now, and if at least one-quarter of women and one-sixth of men experience childhood sexual trauma, then there are likely many more people in this type of marriage who are either wrestling with same-sex attractions, the effects of trauma, or both, like I am.[3] But even if we are different, if we really are just a footnote to "normal" marriages, are we really *so different?*

Is our oneness impossible?

Is our physical oneness impossible? This question still stood before me.

Yes, I had turned and repented from fantasizing about a physical connection within another relationship. I heard from the Holy Spirit and knew that God was calling me to this marriage. I rid myself of my reasons to leave and started taking the half steps I could. I understood that the purpose of marriage is to demonstrate to the world God's love for them. I even got that we along with everyone else "married wrongly," as Tolkien puts it, but were still called to oneness.

But was physical, sexual unity possible with us? Or are we just a footnote of impossibility?

Is there a reason to have sex beyond having kids? Like, really, what's the point?

If left up to me, the answer was easy: no. No to sex in our marriage. We already had a couple of kids—weren't we set?

Sex is a oneness cultivator for married people. It's a gospel metaphor for married people. I could not see this, however, because I was thinking wrongly about physical intimacy completely.

As much as I resented seeing increasing relational closeness in many romantic comedies inevitably leading to a fade-to-black sex scene, this was how I viewed marital intimacy. You get closer emotionally, spiritually, socially and wink wink—it leads to sex. It leads to oneness. Oneness, in my mind, was a euphemism for sex. I could not shake this perspective.

Until I could.

God is three in one. We, the church, are to image God through unity—many people in one. It's like Jesus prayed in the garden, "I pray that they will all be one, just as you and I are one—as you are in me, Father, and I am in you. And may they be in us so that the world will believe you sent me" (John 17:21).

Paul uses the image of a body to communicate this truth: "The human body has many parts, but the many parts make up one whole body. So it is with the body of Christ. . . . All of you together are Christ's body, and each of you is a part of it" (1 Corinthians 12:12, 27). Single people are a part of this body. Married people are a part of this body—not as individual people but as one unit within the body. "They are no longer two but one," Jesus says of married folks (Matthew 19:6). We are two in one.

So, God is three in one. We, the church, are to be many parts in one, and those parts include single people and married people—which are two in one.

Let's dive further into the body metaphor: Matt and I, together, are maybe a cell on the pinky toe. I want you to picture that cell as a mountain. As with all metaphors, this one is imperfect, but bear with me because it has helped us greatly.

Prior to this mountain, Matt and I were once on our own individual mountains before we married. On those mountains, we were also the head gardeners. The ground there was sloped, not steep, and the soil was rich enough for seven gardens to produce seven different types of fruit. When we married, those two mountains became one. Two gardeners moved from their own gardens into shared ones. We covenanted oneness until death do us part, mirroring the forever covenant of oneness Jesus made to us.

And we call this *starting* moment "happily ever after"?

That is hard! This is (dare we say it again?) impossible without Christ.

But let's dive into just how impossible it is without Christ.

Those seven gardens that produce seven different types of fruit have a name. I'm going to call them the Gardens of Relating. Let me walk you through each of the seven:

There's the family garden where we bring in our family of origin seeds (gifts) and weeds (pain), our styles of parenting, and things like distribution of house work.

The social and emotional gardens produce the ways we socially and emotionally relate.

The physical garden includes all of ways we relate physically, but it also includes how we care for our bodies through disciplines like eating, exercising, and sleeping well. This is also the space where we can bring in weeds of sexual sin or physical or sexual trauma.

The stewardship garden cultivates stewardship of our money, time, and what we own. Its fruit is critical as money is one of the primary reasons for divorce.[4]

The spiritual garden is not the only place we relate to God, but in it blooms the primary avenues for connecting with him. It is there that we find the fruit of spiritual disciplines, like prayer, confession, lamentation, and involvement in our local churches.

The intellectual garden is the last garden, and it yields the ways we relate to others with our intellect.

Now, the dream scenario is for husband and wife to perfectly unite all of their gardens. They then take this perfect unity with them as they relate to other gardeners on the mountains around them. As all of them perfectly relate to other mountain ranges throughout the geography of the church, that body then makes disciples together.

But perfect unity is hard. Impossible, actually. The only way for two things to fit together perfectly is for they themselves to be perfect. But we can't be perfect. We just can't—on our own. We need the perfect Gardener, God, to make a way (John 15:1). He did. He does. He not only tells us how to live perfectly through the Word, and he not only demonstrated how we can do so by coming to earth, but Jesus also made a path for us imperfect people to become perfect like him through his death on the cross and sent his Spirit to empower us to live it (Hebrews 10:14, John 16:13).

The weight of perfect gardening is on Jesus. All we have to do is surrender, confess, and say, "I can't. You can through me—through us."

But then we step forward. We learn to walk like he walks. Garden like he gardens. "How would Jesus respond to my spouse here?" "How would he react in this situation?" "Jesus, I can't, will you through me?" We confess when we fail, we celebrate with each other when we don't, and no matter what, we remember the weight of our marriages is on Jesus. We can't. He can. Take a next half step forward with him.

Okay, but what about sex in particular? How does that relate to all of this? Is that just a part of the physical garden?

We're getting there.

On all of our metaphorical mountains, the Holy Spirit sends rain (Matthew 5:45).[5] Married and single gardeners have the same goal: Remove the weeds and cultivate the fruit-bearing seeds so that the Holy Spirit's rain can flow through healthy gardens, insert good nutrients, and produce fruit that tumbles down your mountain to serve and feed the body of Christ.

Every good gift and all empowerment to cultivate is from God, and all we do goes back to God. If our life goal is to image God and point to Jesus, we do this on our mountains.

Let me say it another way: Cultivating our gardens well—mimicking the Gardener, working with our co-gardener (if we are married), inviting others to help us remove weeds and plant good seeds—produces much fruit.

Others can see, feel, and experience this fruit as a witness to the world that God loves them, wants to be one with them, and will one day marry us, the church.

It's often easy to see the fruit of couples who have been married for fifty years and have been working on their Holy Spirit-infused unity for that long. The love, joy, peace, patience, and kindness they share makes many of us sigh with longing. We might think it's for their marriage that we ache, but the sigh comes from somewhere deeper. Somewhere ancient and eternal. It's a sighing for *The Impossible Marriage*, the one only made possible by Jesus.

It is a great mystery.

But back to sex.

Does it only happen in the physical sense? I suppose it can. We can engage in the act of sex and have it take place primarily in the physical garden.[6] Please him. Please her. Done. We married folks can engage in primarily physical-only sex, but please don't call it oneness.

If marriage is a metaphor of our union with God, such body-only sex would be like physically attending church activities while boasting, "I am one with God."

The type of sex that creates oneness takes place in all of the gardens with the Holy Spirit pouring all over it. It may start with an intellectually stimulating conversation in the morning (intellectual garden) followed by a fun date and deep discussion in the afternoon (social and emotional garden), which leads to pursuing each other physically in the evening while considering how best to care for the other person's body in this space. Notice that sex is, well, inexpensive (stewardship garden). In this space, we practice an awareness of God while engaging each other (spiritual garden) and ask if he is calling us to make the fruit of a baby (family garden). Through sex, our gardens can overflow with connection and bear the fruit of oneness.

Let's focus for a minute on the fruit but also on where the water to create it originated: God. Awareness of God in all of this is critical. Our lives come from whom? They are empowered by whom? They are flowing out toward whom? God, God, God! If sex is about sex—about physical gratification—that's boring. That's worldly. Idolatrous. It's both elevating and diminishing sex to where it shouldn't be. Matt elevated sex by thinking it was primarily about physical gratification. I diminished it by thinking it was primarily about physical gratification and an exchange of goods (my body for his heart).

Sex includes our physical gardens, but it is about so much more than that. If a marriage between a man and a woman is a tangible picture of God's marriage to us, that includes sexual intimacy. Why do we forget this? Am I the only one who doesn't automatically link God to sex? But we must. The marriage metaphor doesn't only permeate our covenant, our promises, and our unification of money, time, and friendship, it penetrates our bodies as well.

As a woman is opened to receive a man in her deepest, most sensitive parts, so God wants us to be opened to receive him in the deepest parts of us.

This is a great mystery.

But do you know what? Matt and I have prayed many times before having sex. We did so in the years of me detaching my brain from having sex with him and while he was addicted to porn. Slapping a prayer on sexual intimacy doesn't magically transform it into the gospel metaphor. It doesn't make sex a living, breathing picture of God's desire to tenderly care for, explore, awaken, and know our deepest parts—yes, the physical but also the intellectual, the social, the stewardship . . . all of the gardens totally connected.

Paul writes, "The person who is joined to the Lord is one spirit with him" (1 Corinthians 6:17). This phrase—literally contextualized in a passage about sexual union—goes beyond praying "the prayer" and asking Jesus into your heart. It is a picture of surrendering all of the gardens—every area of our lives.

That is oneness with him. *That* is marriage to him.

That should be marriage oneness with our spouses.

Sex doesn't equal oneness, but sex can be awash in oneness.

I see why people view sex as ultimate. We sense something of oneness when we walk the timeline of deep conversation, laughter during a date, prayer, and voila! At least one of us experiences some level of orgasmic euphoria during sex, so that must be proof that sex is ultimate.

No, it isn't. Sex—even the best oneness-lathered, Holy Spirit–filled, metaphor-rich, gospel-breathing sex—is fasting compared to what true union with the Father will feel like.

C. S. Lewis says it best by comparing our lack of understanding this heavenly euphoria to explaining sex to a prepubescent kid for the first time. We say, "It's great!" but the greatest object he knows at his age is chocolate. So, he asks, "Is there chocolate with sex?" When he hears, "No," he is disappointed.

> The boy knows chocolate: he does not know the positive thing that excludes it. We are in the same position. We know the sexual life; we do not know, except in glimpses, the other thing which, in Heaven, will leave no room for it. Hence where fullness awaits us, we anticipate fasting.[7]

If we stare at sex to meet a soul need in us, we will be left starving for more (2 Peter 2:19).

If we diminish sex to a physical-only event, we will miss out on experiencing a gospel-rich metaphor.

If we look through the metaphor of sex to see it as a message God wants to send to us and to our spouses of his desire for holistic union with us, sex can be good. A fraction of the ultimate good but good.

As a same-sex attracted, trauma-scarred woman who is called to be married to a man, I can get excited about sex when it's talked about this way.

God wants to tell me, Matt, and the world that he loves us, and he can use the fruit of oneness-drenched sex to spread that message.

Maybe sexual intimacy in our marriage wasn't a footnote of impossibility after all.

• • •

MATT

Sexual intimacy still felt impossible.

This was good for me to experience. If Laurie was learning that sex was a gift, I was learning that the gift was not ultimate.

Although we were not having sex, we were experiencing oneness, increasingly so. The best place for us was on one of our favorite walks. A five-mile loop weaving through neighborhoods and nature gave us a couple of hours of connection time.

If we opened up our awareness to the Holy Spirit's raining presence, we could work with him to see each of the Gardens of Relating overflow with the fruit of oneness while walking.

Side by side, we often laughed together (social garden), talked about fears and joys (emotional garden), engaged in theories we were working on (intellectual garden), and noticed the walk never cost more than a cup of coffee (stewardship garden). We were together as a family (family garden), we often prayed as we walked (spiritual garden), and because we were physically caring for our bodies by walking or if Laurie held my hand even for a short while, it tapped the physical garden.

If you would see us after we went for a great walk, our faces might be aglow. We may appear like ... well, like something sexual had happened. But it hadn't.

Oneness is not a euphemism for sex.

Oneness is Holy Spirit-fueled unity in all of the areas of relating.

I needed to know this. Sex is a gift. It is a gospel metaphor. It can be awash in oneness, but it's not the only path to it. Walking can lead to oneness. So can co-teaching on a stage, podcasting together, serving others, and raising kids side by side.

Putting sex in the context of this metaphor helped me to better understand why I idolized sex and why Laurie diminished it.

But we need to add Core Needs into this conversation.

If the mountain, its gardens, and the fruit highlight oneness, Core Needs help us to understand some of our issues with unity.

Let's rewind for a reminder of the ten Core Needs:

Affirmed: overwhelmingly approved of
Desired: specially chosen; no pretense necessary
Included: wanted in this group, team, or partnership; feeling
    "I belong"
Loved: unconditionally accepted
Nurtured: cared for, held
Purposed: filled with a sense of profoundly mattering
Rested: re-centered and reset in mind, body, spirit; includes
    having fun
Delighted in: seen as unique and special
Protected: unafraid; trusting everything is under control
Noticed: seen inside and out

Ideally, God meets our Core Needs with creation supporting the process.

On our metaphorical mountain, these needs are like aqueducts. They are channels that fill with Holy Spirit water, we drink from them, and then the water keeps moving on to the rest of the garden. Each channel fills a different part in our hearts. But it's important to remember that each gardener brings all ten Core Needs to every garden.

The needs are filled a few different ways. The first is easy. We watch the Holy Spirit directly supply water into one of our aqueducts. Let's say it's the *loved* aqueduct in the family garden. We drink it and smile, looking up at God and saying, "Thank you. I feel loved by you." It feels simple. It may come through reading a verse or hearing that still, small voice in our hearts, but it feels direct and barrier-free. God pours out his love, and we drink it.

Other times, we have to work for it by toiling with the kids all day, cleaning at night, and trying to parent like God. And in the middle of that pain, we sense his love. "Good job," he says, and we sigh. "Thank you." It's not as easy; there are some barriers, but it's still quite direct. God pours out his love, and after a bit of effort, we reach out to scoop it up and drink it.

The third way is through our co-gardener or other gardeners on mountains nearby. We may toil all day in the family garden but struggle to see God's love. A friend notices a blockage on this aqueduct and helps to move it. "I know you feel God doesn't notice you because your children are ungrateful, but he sees your hard work even when they don't. He isn't looking away." Ah, there it is: sweet water. "Thank you," we say, drinking from the newly cleared *loved* aqueduct.

The physical garden has been the most challenging for Laurie and me to cultivate. "Of course, it is," people say to both of us. "Matt, you married the wrong person. Laurie, you outright married the wrong gender." But if marriage in God's eyes is between a man and a woman, if Laurie was called to marriage and, therefore, called to marry a man, if we all truly marry the wrong person, how can our physical interaction be possible?

Let's look at some of the problem areas in our marriage's physical garden: weeds. We both brought in junk from our past sins. She had memories. I had memories. We've both had to confess sin and allow God's forgiveness to set us free from condemnation and shame.

Laurie also brought in trauma. It often feels like a giant boulder between us, too heavy to move. We believe it's not, but it can feel that way.

We also carried into this garden our default sexual brokenness of lust toward women. Both of us. Of course, sexual brokenness isn't only housed in this physical garden, but it often affects it quite a bit.

Into this garden we also carry good things—seeds of relating physically to each other, to our kids, and to others. Everyone has their own unique style of physical connection, and it is beautiful and necessary.

The last thing we carry into each garden are those Core Need aqueducts that can get blocked so easily. In this intersection between needs and gardens we find Laurie and my false views of physically relating—seeing it as either ultimate or worthless.

So, Core Needs: there are ten, but let's focus on the need to be *protected*. As I look around the physical garden, it is often easy for me to feel protected here. I'm a heterosexual dude, right? The physical kingdom should be my domain, unless my ability to choose is gone.

I felt this sometimes while growing up. As I mentioned already, my mom was a wonderful woman, but she was broken. She worked tirelessly to communicate to my brother and me that she loved us. She did so by serving us, affirming us, and by giving many hugs. As I grew older—especially into later adolescence—I began to refuse my mother's attempted embrace. It wasn't until after I had been married for a few years that I could pinpoint why hugging my mom felt so different. She constantly wanted it. Every time I drove back to college, she asked for multiple hugs on the way to the car and then reached in through the window for another before I left. This persistent pressure felt less like an invitation and more like a demand. A good need in my mom to be noticed or affirmed became a requirement. It became an idol. Instead of looking through me to God to meet this need in her, it felt like she just looked *to* me. I instinctively felt this sinful switch, although I could not name it until years later.

This physical memory can become a barrier in my ability to get my need to be protected met in the physical garden. If I don't feel I can say no, if I feel as if the touch I'm receiving isn't actually for me, an alarm sounds in my head, and I don't feel safe.

I also bring my primary Core Need to be desired into this garden. It is also the primary the reason I can make physically relating ultimate. I feel the need to be desired and then ask, "Laurie, do you desire me?" Lately, I have been training myself to ask instead, "God, do you desire me?" I cannot bring this empty need to Laurie to fill. When I bring my empty desires to Laurie instead of looking through her to God who desires me, I will inevitably seek my own fulfillment rather than serving my wife like Christ serves the church (Ephesians 5:25).

Doing so is sinful. It is sinful to allow a good need to become a demand (an idol), by requiring a human to fill it. It's what my mom did to me. I don't want to pass it on.

It is also critical for me to realize that God wants to meet this good need to be desired in me—but not only in the physical garden. He wants to fill it in the emotional, the social, and the family gardens. "I want to be with you, Matt," God can say to me through friendships. "I pursue your heart," he can say in an emotional conversation with my wife. "I want you!" he can say through my kids.

For too many years, I was a one garden man with a one Core Need song to sing. "Desire me, Laurie," I sang. "In this physical way," I crooned. She couldn't satiate that need in me, so I turned to porn. "Desire me in this way," I sang to a screen. I hoped the good need was filling up with Holy Spirit water, but it was actually filling with pebbles. Therefore, I added more barriers between my good need and the God who can meet it because that's what sin does.

But I could help remove safety barriers for Laurie. I could help her see she could choose. We had already taken sex off the table, but in this season of working intensely on our marriage connection, I needed to remove any physical touch that felt to her as if I were taking, even if it didn't feel like taking to me.

Whenever I saw Laurie drained emotionally, I wanted to silently give her a hug. "I love you," I intended the hug to say. But a silent hug can say something much different to someone who has experienced silent, physical trauma. It can speak, "I take from you," and I didn't want to communicate that. I am her co-gardener, not her assailant.

So when I noticed her cringing at my hugs, I realized her need to be protected was blocked. "How can I help you to feel safe?" I asked.

"Say something," she suggested. "Tell me you love me; don't automatically hug me. If you really want to tell me you love me through a hug, please ask. If I say yes, face me as you do so. I need to see your eyes."

As I engaged her in this way, I was surprised to find that she seemed more open to me physically. As I cared for her need to be protected in this garden, she seemed more able to lean into hugging me—into cultivating this physical place with me.

Yippee for me! It's go time! I could think. *Nope. Stop, Matt. Stop.* Anytime this dynamic happened, anytime I worked with the Gardener to remove barriers between her need to be protected and the God who meets that need, I had to stop the train. I had to look at my need to be desired in this physical garden and talk to it.

"She is not my idol. God desires me. Look through her to him." If I didn't do this, if I got carried away with glee that she finally wanted to hug me, I watched the rocks that I worked so hard to remove pile back on. She didn't feel protected—and rightly so— because I wasn't looking through her to God who desires me. Instead, I was looking to her to fill that need.

This is exactly where my desires for sex can become ultimate—where my good need to be desired becomes an idol.

How brilliant is God to bring Laurie and me together in marriage to refine some of our core issues so terribly and perfectly?

One of her weakest places is feeling *protected* in the physical garden. One of my weakest places is being *desired* in the physical garden. These weaknesses have the potential to tear us apart and leave our marriage in tatters, but they also provide us with an opportunity to work together to remove the barriers that keep us from seeing it is God who *protects* and *desires* us. Our weakest places can become our strongest if we cultivate with God in the garden.

Before we turn the page on our metaphorical mountain, I want to make sure we get this concept with one more example from a mountain nearby. Zoom out from our mountain and you'll see a nearby mountain where two of our friends reside.

Each of them differ from us in terms of their primary Core Needs. They also have different problem gardens and different ways of fostering sex awash in oneness. His primary Core Need is to be *affirmed* in the stewardship garden—specifically stewarding his gifts at his job. Hers is to be *noticed*—specifically in the family garden. A lack of oneness for them often occurs when he gets home from work.

If he doesn't jump quickly into cultivating the family garden alongside her—wrangling kids, noticing the delicious meal she made, and practically helping to make sure everything is rolling in her often-forgotten world of parenting—a barrier builds up over her need to be *noticed*. Now, she could barrel through, look up at Jesus, and say, "God, do you *notice* me? I'm feeling forgotten." Doing so would allow her to drink deeply from that aqueduct all day, but she often doesn't. (Do many of us?) Instead, she says, "You don't see me," upon her husband's arrival home. "You don't even care what I do. I work so hard with these kids, and you come home and act like one of them!"

Ouch. But common, right? The husband, after a dreary, hard day might think, "Ugh. Again. She doesn't ever *affirm* me." He may also think, "No sex tonight because, of course, I failed her again." But sex is the wrong reward. The motivator for their verbal unity needs to not be sex but oneness. Holistic body, soul, spirit unity— whether or not sex is a part of it.

With the metaphorical mountain in mind, my friends may be able to reach a more unified place like this: She has a tough day with the kids, but from morning until evening she seeks to look up the mountain. "God, do you see me here? Do you love me?" That simple, repetitive act removes some barriers between her good need and the God who meets it.

Meanwhile, her husband is doing the same thing at work. Throughout the day, he brings his need to be *affirmed* to Jesus. "God? Do you *affirm* me? Do you see me right now in this job I don't love? My gifts feel wasted. Can you speak encouraging words here?" That simple, repetitive act removes some barriers between his good need and the God who meets it.

Then he comes home. Either could go first, but maybe this time she says, "Hey, honey. How are you? How was work? I'm sure it was hard not to get away from the desk all day, huh?" Because her husband has been seeking God since that morning, her *affirmation* of him is not his life. It simply adds to the *affirmation* need that has been getting filled by the giver of life.

He goes next. "Hey, honey. Wow, it looks like you were super involved with the kids today. That must have been hard and fun. How can I help with dinner?" Because she has been seeking God all day, his *noticing* of her does not become her life. It simply adds to the *noticed* need that has been getting filled by the giver of life.

Oneness. Their unity may lead to sex later, but it doesn't have to. What matters most is they are seeking to be one with each other like God seeks to be one with us.

This is hard. The work is no joke.

If Jesus could give up his life to be one with us, what more can we give up in order to be increasingly one with each other?

Good grief. If our metaphorical mountain is anything like real life, it highlights for me the magnitude of the challenge to connect.

The challenge can make us feel like we married the wrong person. It can make us feel like our marriage is impossible.

We sure did. It sure is.

Without Christ. But when he's present? When we are working with the Gardener to weed, seed, remove boulders, and remove barriers between him and our needs? That oneness is something to behold.

It's a gorgeous, overflowing harvest of oneness.

SIX

THE AWKWARD MIDDLE

The whole life of the good Christian is a holy
longing. . . . That is our life, to be trained by longing.

SAINT AUGUSTINE

LAURIE

I was starting to get it: the purpose of marriage, the purpose of sex, the intentional beauty of oneness in marriage.

But the answers were like a book in my hand—a book I begrudgingly read and understood—and I still had to peer over the top at my life. *Does this really apply to me? It must. If God is Creator and I am a created being, my life makes the most sense in alignment with his . . . good design.* I was still getting used to the idea that sex was good—a good metaphor.

But how the heck do I make it work in real life? God, if you have called me to this marriage, if you have called me to tangibly share your love with Matt, help me. I'm not asking you to turn me straight. I'm asking you to make me one with Matt. Not men—Matt.

My brain got it, but my heart didn't. Yes, there was the sexual orientation thing, but I had a sense that it was the trauma blocking me more than my sexual desires.

It felt like a rock in my chest. I had even named it: The Memory. It felt like the greatest issue in our impossible marriage. I had tried everything to remove it. I exhausted every tool in my kit trying to wedge it free. I attended counseling, signed up for marriage intensives, talked it through with friends, quieted my mind through contemplative prayer, all in an attempt to force my way into the memory and remove its power over me. *Maybe if God would show me exactly what happened, I could invite him into that space and see how he was truly there the whole time. I could be liberated from the Memory's heavy, dark grip with his light.* I had done similar practices with other dark memories before and found success. *Why are none of my old tools working? What is it going to take to get you to move, God?*

Months were turning into years of hardly any physical connection with Matt, but this rock of my past didn't budge.

God can heal me, I thought, *but he won't. Maybe this is my life. I won't ever get better.*

It wouldn't have mattered so much—this memory wedged in my chest—if I didn't have a husband. He was the one who triggered me. His presence along with the birth of our daughter woke this memory in me and forced me to confront it. However, I couldn't confront it. I couldn't remove it. I just had to live with it.

"Why did God make me remember pieces of this?" I bemoaned to my therapist. "If I could take a pill to forget it all again I would."

"But, Laurie," she said slowly, "whether or not you remembered, the rock was still there. It was still affecting your life. You just didn't know it."

I couldn't argue with her. Ever since it happened, the Memory had been there, lying dormant and unprocessed. Matt didn't put the rock there—my assailant did. He just brought it to my attention. If I had the eyes to see, I would thank God that he had called me to marriage with a man because in doing so, he invited me into deeper healing of my soul.

But this memory was causing my body to live in what felt like a constant state of panic. When people go through trauma, the memory is "stored" in their bodies. Bessel van der Kolk, a clinician and researcher of post-traumatic stress disorder, explores this in his book *The Body Keeps the Score*. On this body storage process he said:

The core issue with trauma is that people feel unsafe in their bodies. Your body keeps reacting right now as if you're still in danger, right now. The degree to which your body keeps reacting that way defines the depth of your trauma . . . So, trauma is really a bodily state of feeling deeply uncomfortable, hyperaroused, or not feeling anything at all.[1]

Traumatized people can feel uncomfortable, hyperaroused, or numbed out in the present, even though the pain happened in the past. Trauma is so traumatic that our brains rewire to over-react mentally and bodily even years later.

Our stress hormones are meant to help us move, or fight back, and get out of the situation. If they keep being se-creted [because the victim is held down or unable to move for some reason], they keep you in a state of hyperarousal or put you in a state of helpless collapse. When this happens over time, the filtering system of the brain is changed so you become hypersensitive to certain sounds. You have dif-ficulty filtering irrelevant information. Gradually, you start feeling threat everywhere. Instead of being focused on what is going on right now, your mind stays on the alert for threat, while you basically feel helpless to do anything about it.[2]

This constant alertness in our minds affects our very cells. Van der Kolk and Harvard researchers conducted a study of women who had been traumatized alongside women who had not and found an abnormality in the women who had been trau-matized in their CD45 cells. These are memory and replicator cells that can "remember" danger. They found that the cells in the traumatized women were hyperactive—much like our hyperaroused brains. "They dig up too much danger," van der Kolk said. They identified threat where none existed. "The whole organism is traumatized," he said, noting that several of *only* the traumatized women had hyperactive CD45 cells, which had developed autoimmune diseases in the women.[3]

We are holistic creatures and trauma affects everything from our brains to our very cells . . . for a long time.

Mentally, theologically, I got it. Matt's desire for me physically was a good thing. When his eyes or words said, "I love you, I want to be with you," I learned to translate his desire. *He is reflecting God's desire to be with me. Matt's physical desire is one way God says, "I am, I want to, and I will be totally one with you."*

But bodily—in the places where this rock of a memory was stored—I didn't get it. I saw trauma where there was none.

I still froze. Matt still triggered me, and nothing I did seemed to change that. Had I not been married, had I not had this calling on my life to be one with this man, I would have been able to cope better.

God knows the best way to bless and perfect us—whether we're single or married.

Marriage was God's call for me, but as a married person there is another person, my co-gardener, who is very affected by my wounding.

"How are you doing with all of this?" I asked Matt one morning.

"I talked about it to God last night," Matt said, sighing. "I asked him if he ever feels like I do." He looked up at the ceiling. "'Every day,' I heard. God feels rejected by his people every day. 'Everyone would rather run to something other than me.'"

I tried not to turn Matt's words into a knife cutting up my soul, but it felt too hard. *See, Laurie? You're such a freak. You're irrevocably broken. Look at his eyes. You are injuring this good man.*

"It hurts to hear that," I said bitterly. "It's great God has compassion on you, but what about me? That puts me in the adulterer spot."

So often, I felt that Matt was the perfect God character and I was Hosea's wife. I was Israel. I was the cheater with the wayward attractions, the permanently broken one. Of course, I knew that

Matt understood I was in frozen pain over this memory. *But why does he have to say how he feels?*

Because I had asked. Because he matters. Because *he isn't God.* He is a person. He's allowed to feel, and I simply perpetuated his childhood wounding when I silenced his emotions and voice.

"I am allowed to feel," Matt gently reminded me several times in that season. *Yes, he is allowed to feel,* I had to tell myself. *Stop panicking. God sees your pain. You affect Matt. That's okay. You are not abandoned.*

But right here, in this sort of moment—where I see how imperfect I am and experience another person affected by my brokenness—is where I face my greatest temptation: to get my need for *protection* met on my own.

The need for *protection* bubbles to the surface when Matt says, "I'm in pain too." My wounds wound him, and I feel bad about that. I feel unstable. Unsafe. Instead of staying, engaging, and feeling the cost my pain inflicts on him like a grownup, I choose the easy and childish route.

"I know how to get this need to be safe met," I think. "I'll run away." So I shut my mouth and isolate. *I will protect myself. I will keep myself safe by being alone. If I am silent and alone, I can't hurt anyone.*

But you know what? If I try to get my heart needs met in ways outside of God and his good design, it's not going to work. God designed me to be in relationship. So, as I isolate, as I run away to my own corner of our metaphorical mountain, I feel pseudo-protected. But I'm not. Things start to die because I neglect my gardening responsibilities with my husband and the gardeners around me on other mountains.

When I try to hide my needs from people, weeds start growing in the Gardens of Relating. Rocks start piling up over the Core Needs. We need the body of Christ to help uproot weeds and remove barriers from needs.

Could God meet all of these needs without the help of people if I were sick or incapacitated in some way? Absolutely. But *I* had made the choice to isolate. *I had chosen* to walk away to my own corner of the mountain, and everything started to die.

That's not his design for us.

Then what can take away this aching in my chest? I wanted to give up.

Every day, I imagined stepping in front of a car. *I just want to die. That will end all the pain.* Thoughts of death assaulted me constantly.

In the middle of this darkness, God inevitably broke through. He used the voice of a friend, a verse from the Bible, or a whisper to my soul that woke me up. *He's with me. He loves me. I don't want to die.* He filled me with hope.

However, I didn't stop in that awkward place in the middle of my suffering and stare at him as my protector, the One who sees me and gives me a place to belong. Instead, I often rode the pendulum to the opposite side of self-inflicted isolation.

Friends will meet my need to belong. Fantasizing about a woman will satisfy this aching need to be seen. Maybe Matt can fix my desire to be included—if only he would stop sharing his own pain. How about a pan of brownies to satisfy this need for nurture? Maybe if I get enough likes online, I'll feel delighted in. Perhaps securing that one speaking gig will help me feel like I have purpose.

But inevitably either the world and people failed me or I failed them. Then I didn't feel safe, and I isolated again . . . and it led to despair.

Extremism: All people, all of the world, all of the time. Or no people, no part of the world, any part of the time.

There is hardly ever a time when extremism is the right choice.

Christopher West, a student and expert of John Paul II's *Theology of the Body,* has a name for these extreme options. The isolated person is the "stoic." They feel their desire but silence it. The "addict" tries to suck infinity out of the finite world. The ideal disciple—the one who suffers well—is the "mystic."

The *mystic* is the one who allows himself to feel the deepest depths of human desire and chooses to "stay in the pain" of wanting more than this life has to offer. Having walked through many purifying trials (what the mystical tradition of the Church calls "dark nights"), he is able both to do without the many pleasures of this world *and* to rejoice in all the true pleasures of this world without idolizing them— that is, without trying to suck infinity out of them. As the Apostle Paul says, "I have learned the secret of being well fed and of going hungry, of living in abundance and of being in need." (Phil. 4:12)[4]

God invites us into the uncomfortable, painful, growth-stirring middle.

"Don't be extreme, dear one," I heard. "Sit in the uncomfortable center. Feel the pain you are causing Matt. Don't run from him. Feel the pain this memory is causing you. Don't run from it. Grip me in the middle of this suffering. Look *through* people and this world to me. Not *to* people and this world instead of me. Not *from* people and this world to nothing."

It's in this place of gripping God in the midst of suffering that I am the most *protected* because I am walking in God's will. Protection doesn't mean I will never experience suffering. It means my soul will be safe in the midst of suffering (Proverbs 18:10).

One evening, God called me back from one of my pendulum swings toward isolation. Matt had been opening up about his pain in a tender way, and I shut down like a child. *Fine. Who cares? I hurt him. I can't control this. I'm just going to go to sleep.* I slammed my sleep mask over my eyes and let myself internally fall off of a depressed, isolated cliff as I fell asleep.

But God nudged me awake.

"Where is your little girl?" The Holy Spirit whispered. My therapist taught me how little girl Laurie was the one triggered by Matt—not the adult. When we experience trauma, a part of us gets stuck at that age we were traumatized.[5] "She is the one terrified of him and who wants to isolate from him. Not your adult self," my counselor had said. At first, it sounded like she was speaking a foreign language: I, adult Laurie, was not afraid of Matt. I, adult Laurie, didn't want to isolate from him. I loved him and chose him.

Yes. Right. Got it.

She wasn't wrong. The translation just took a lot of effort.

"You must learn to have compassion on her," she said of my little girl inside. "Love and care for her." Again, a foreign language. Little Laurie annoyed me. She was keeping me from living my best life by reliving trauma from a memory I couldn't remember. But God and my therapist seemed to be working together.

"Where is she?" God whispered again.

I searched inside for Little Laurie.

I could see her. Underneath my childish default to run and isolate, Little Laurie was screaming inside of a large, stone room with a white, concrete floor. Bright, invasive lights caused her to hide her face in her arms. My anger was covering my fear.

"What is she saying?"

I took a deep breath and envisioned adult Laurie approaching her. "Get away! Get away from me! I don't want anyone," she cried, alone and lonely.

"Tell Matt."

What? No. I'll sound stupid. He's reading anyway.

"Tell him where she is and what she is saying."

Fine.

I left my sleep mask on, determined to go to sleep after this. "Matt, my little girl inside is screaming, 'Get away. Get away from me. I don't want anyone.' She is in a room alone." Done. Goodnight, Jesus.

"Ask him to invite his little boy to come talk with you there."

That. Is. Dumb. No counselor told us to do that. I don't even know if that's a thing we're supposed to do! It might damage me further.

I remembered something I said earlier in the week: "Our marriage intensive counselor may not have his master's in counseling, but the Holy Spirit has one hundred million doctoral degrees. God can use anything or anyone he chooses because he is God."

Fine!

"Matt, can you have your little boy talk to my little girl inside?" Just the thought of it—the thought of kindness to this little girl inside—and tears poured from my eyes.

"Okay," he said, putting his book aside. I could tell he felt somewhat awkward, but our lives were already so shaken up from the norm by the Memory that he was willing to try anything. "How do you want me to do that?"

I plowed forward through my fear and need for *protection.* "Just talk to me."

"Okay," he took a deep breath and closed his eyes. "Hi."

"Hi," I said.

I could see little boy Matt: an eight-year-old with a brown-blond scraggly haircut—a clean mullet like he wore for a few years as a boy. He had battered knees visible below his too-big T-shirt and shorts.

As I looked down at me, I could see myself at about eight too. My pink and purple shorts were also too large and my thick bangs needed a trim. Tears cut lines through my dirty face. I felt around inside my chest and could tell I felt alone, lost in this bright dungeon of a room.

But Matt said, "Hi." I wasn't alone. My best friend was here! My heart knew him. Somehow, I lost him, but I also knew him. I smiled in real life, wiped real tears away. And so did the eight-year-old inside. I was grateful my friend was here. Not my assailant. Not my enemy. Not a man. Not someone who wanted to hurt me. A boy. A boy-friend.

"Do you want to play a game?" I asked.

"Sure! Let's play Heave-Ho," Matt said, winking at me through this strange place we were in. "Heave-Ho" was our oldest daughter's name for tug of war. I laughed, then grew quiet.

"I don't like this place," I said, hearing fear in my voice.

"No?"

"No, it's cold. And scary."

"Do you want to go somewhere else?"

I did.

"Where are the cats?" He asked. He winked at me again in this strange world by referring to a place in my mind I often go to pray with God. It was a real place I often hid as a child, but now I go back mentally to feel safe and protected with God when I pray.

I flew there in my mind, to a field behind a large house my family owned for a few years. It had a pond I often sat by to get away from the noise of big-family living. As an introvert, I needed it. In the summers I used to hunt for stray kittens that escaped from neighboring farms. I caught them using borrowed cans of tuna from the kitchen and even convinced my parents to let me keep one as an outdoor friend.

"I see some over there!" I laughed between the tears, glad to be away from the harsh and lonely room.

Matt laughed, too, reaching out to me as he did. He was telling me he knows these sacred places no one else knows. He saw me. He *delighted* in me. He was reflecting God's seeing and *delighting* in me. "They are so cute," he chuckled.

"I like this place." We said only simple sentences, but there was much meaning beneath them.

"Want to sit next to the pond?"

He did.

"I like the reeds," he said. I could hear them rustling. "What do you like about it here today?"

"The quiet and peace. I want to lay down and look up at the clouds—find shapes in them. Want to join me?" I could sense him lying back next to me in the grass in his mind. We looked up at the clouds and sighed. I still felt the pain of the Memory between us, still felt its weight in my chest. But I wasn't running. I was letting Matt into a place in my heart where I was hiding and feeling the most shame—it did something in me.

As we lay there in our real bed—a place laden with so much pain and shame—but mentally lying next to each other in nature, sun on our faces, looking up at the perfect, puffy, clouded sky, listening to reeds, cuddling kittens . . . we connected. Awkwardly, yes, but I shockingly felt safe. Protected. Seen. All the Core Needs seemed to fill as I stayed in the awkward middle, enjoying this moment.

We stayed there awhile, looking up at the sky, exchanging stories about our favorite pets. His dogs, Blitz and Bolt. My dog, Belle. Those kittens. We shed real tears over losing them. Little Matt and Little Laurie became closer friends, and so did the adults. Unprompted, I reached out for his hand.

He squeezed mine back, winking at me again. *I know this is hard,* he seemed to say. *But you're not alone. You don't have to be alone here.*

I still wanted to run. I still wanted to escape—to isolation, a woman, food, curling up in a ball and hiding—but I also didn't. I knew it led to more despair. More emptiness.

Staying was harder. Opening up my heart felt awkward. But because it was so hard it forced me to grip a stronger hand through it. It forced me recognize the Giver in the midst of the gift.

It felt awkward, but it also felt right.

• • •

MATT

I needed a haircut. My dark, coarse hair does not grow down as it gets longer but sideways and up. It's more like a plant than hair, and it was time to prune the plant.

I was grateful for the excuse for some time alone. I felt I needed the space away from work, away from the kids, and away from . . . Laurie. Although she had grown in many ways, growth isn't always a straight walk up a mountain. There were days and hours when I felt she had regressed. Her jaw tensed and her back went rigid when I walked in a room. Our conversations were kind, practical, and schedule-related but without relational exploration.

We had recently had a sweet and strange interchange between Little Laurie and Little Matt, but those connections weren't often. She was struggling to stay present in this awkward middle place with me, God, and her pain.

When she iced me out, I thought, *Here we are again. Back to emotional and physical isolation.* It felt like moving through wet concrete to shift my focus from her to God. Without realizing it, as I watched and waited for her to get better, my staring and waiting turned Laurie into an idol. *Return to God,* I told myself. *Eyes on him, Matt. Stay present. Stay in the awkward middle. God is working on her heart. He's working on yours too. Be thankful you are growing.*

In my worst moments of my worst days, I did not refocus on God with gratitude. I did not want him to be my sustenance. I did not want to do all this work. I wanted my life back. I wanted comfort. Other married couples did not seem to have to work so hard. Why did we?

As I walked into the hair salon, I saw that my regular hair cutter was working. "Hey!" she said over her shoulder, working on someone else's style. "I'm sorry. I'm booked solid today."

"It's okay," I replied, feeling a little sad. I began making arrangements to have the woman at the desk cut my hair. She took me back to her open haircut station to prep me for my pruning.

As we passed my usual hairstylist, I caught a glimpse of her watching me in the mirror. "Try to make an appointment next time," she said over her shoulder. But as she said it, her face seemed sad. I paused. *She wants to be with me,* I thought. *She wants to be in my presence.*

Her warmth was a sharp contrast to the cold of our home.

I had not seen such a look of desire on Laurie's face in months. It didn't seem like a sexual gaze but one that was kind. Warm. Inviting. It lacked the brittle edge of fear covered by anger I experienced almost every day.

I felt something . . . a draw toward her. It felt nice that she was disappointed, even if she only wanted to cut my hair.

No, Matt, I said to myself as the new hair stylist wrapped the protective cape around my neck. *Don't go there.* My mind had begun to wander, taking the innocent look she had given me as a starting place for lust. *Stop.* I thought. *Stop.*

This is how my sexual brokenness reveals itself: I feel the good Core Needs inside of me—to be *protected, desired,* and *noticed*—and if I live on autopilot, I take those needs not to God but to sexual connection. To the physical garden. The old melody started playing in my heart: "Desire me," it invited me to sing to her. "In this way," it asked me to croon.

But the answer was not for me to stare in the stylist's mirror and sing about Laurie. That would simply be another form of idolatry. Nor was my answer to go home, half confess to Laurie about the woman I saw and desired while blaming Laurie for being so cold. "If you would do your marital duty, I wouldn't be struggling this bad. You need to help me reel in my lust."

Because God has given married couples the gift of sex, Laurie *can* help me, but she does not *have* to help me.

If I had a dollar for the number of times I hear these sorts of demands in counseling sessions between married couples, I would be a very rich man. A spouse desires deeper emotional or physical intimacy and blames the other's inability to provide it as the reason their life is imperfect—or the reason they outright cheated. Some, who desire more physical connection, point to 1 Corinthians 7:3-5 as their biblical reasoning:

> The husband should fulfill his wife's sexual needs, and the wife should fulfill her husband's needs. The wife gives authority over her body to her husband, and the husband gives authority over his body to his wife. Do not deprive each other of sexual relations, unless you both agree to refrain from sexual intimacy for a limited time so you can give yourselves more completely to prayer. Afterward, you

should come together again so that Satan won't be able to tempt you because of your lack of self-control.

But those who do miss that the command is reflexive. "Do not deprive each other." Paul is looking at both husband and wife and saying, "Watch yourself. Are you depriving yourself from the other on purpose?" He is not saying, "Make sure the other is not depriving you." He's saying, "Check *yourself*."

Laurie was not intentionally withholding from me. And even if she was, it wasn't my job to force her to engage with me physically. That would be rape. Neither can I blame her for my sin. How would that shake down in the court of God?

God! She wouldn't give to me sexually, so I had to lust. I had to look at porn. I had to have an affair.

Do you think God would buy that—me blaming my wife for my sin? Can we *ever* point to suffering as an excuse for sin?

My suffering was to not have sex. My suffering was to live in a house with a wife who relived her childhood trauma on the regular and, as a result, did not trust me. My suffering was to have a wife who was not naturally sexually attracted to me.

It was hard.

It was not impossible—with God's help.

But I had to turn to him. *I can't do this, God!*

"What? Live without sex?"

Yes! I can't do it.

"Really, Matt? Really? That is your unbearable, impossible suffering?"

In that argument, he often brought to mind a sobering story I read in a book called *The Insanity of God* by Nik Ripkin. The pages tell true tales of the persecuted church from the last few decades. One man's testimony of praising God in the midst of torture arrested me.

The man's name was Dmitri, and he was arrested for starting a house church in communist Russia. He said that what was worse than the physical torture he endured for nineteen years in prison was his physical separation from the body of Christ.

He wanted and needed that oneness.

But God was faithful. Two spiritual practices kept Dimitri connected to God. The first was that every morning, he, the lone believer in a prison of fifteen hundred criminals, would wake up, face the east, and sing words of praise from his aching, longing heart to the one who delighted in him. The other prisoners would bang their cups on the iron bars in angry protest and throw food and human waste to try to shut him up.

The second discipline Dmitri engaged in was to collect scraps of paper in his cell. On each one, he would write a verse or song he knew with a stub of a pencil or a piece of charcoal and place it high up on a moist concrete pillar in his cell as a love offering to God. Inevitably, the guards would find them and beat him severely.

These practices went on year after year until the guards almost broke him. When he was told his wife and sons were dead, he agreed to sign a false confession that he did not believe in Jesus and that he was working for the West to take down the USSR. However, the night before he was to sign it, God allowed Dmitri to hear the real, fervent prayers of his wife and sons while he slept. He knew they were not dead. They were alive and still seeking Jesus. "You lied to me!" he said to his captors. "I am not signing anything!" He continued singing with fervor and writing on scraps of paper as praise to the living God.

Soon after, he found a whole sheet of paper in the prison yard. "And God had laid a pencil beside it!" Dmitri said. Back in his cell, he frantically wrote as much of the Bible as he could and stuck the entire sheet of paper on the wet concrete pillar. When the guards saw it, he was beaten and threatened with execution. As he was being dragged to his death, something amazing happened:

> Before they reached the door leading to the courtyard—
> before stepping out into the place of execution—fifteen
> hundred hardened criminals stood at attention by their
> beds. They faced the east and they began to sing. Dmitri
> told me that it sounded to him like the greatest choir in all

of human history. Fifteen hundred criminals raised their arms and began to sing the HeartSong that they had heard Dmitri sing to Jesus every morning for all of those years.[6]

His jailors, terrified, let go of him. "Who are you?" they asked. "I am a son of the living God," Dmitri responded, shoulders back and head high. "And Jesus is his name!"

Dmitri was returned to his cell and released soon after to his family.

And I'm complaining about not having sex with my wife.

Now, pain is pain. As a therapist, I hear every level of suffering. It all matters to me and to God. I really was struggling in this sexless marriage, but it helped to think about others, such as Dmitri. *This is hard. God sees my pain. But if Dmitri can do that and love Jesus, I can do this and love Jesus.*

Paul wrote to the first-century church, which faced circumstances similar to Dmitri's, and held believers to a high standard when it came to sin. Even in their situation, he commanded them to remain free from sexual immorality. Run from it. Put it to death.[7]

If Dmitri could praise God with a piece of paper in the midst of torture, if the first century church was held to a high standard in the midst of their persecution, I could give up my desires for sex in a tense home.

I could suffer well.

As I left the salon, I breathed deeply, asking God for forgiveness. *I am sorry for letting my mind wander. I am sorry for not suffering well and just whining. I want you. I want to want you more. I feel so lonely in my marriage. I often feel despised in my own home. Please, show me you desire me. You want me. Meet these needs.*

• • •

It was in this season and space that Laurie and I learned how to support each other better in our wrestling with temptation.

When we are in a tough place of temptation, we never want to share with the other person.

Because of what Jesus did for us, we don't need to be so anxious about it. Pastor and author Milton Vincent asks, "Why would anyone be shocked to hear of my struggles with past and present sin when the Cross already told them I am a desperately sinful person?"[8]

Still, vulnerability is terrifying, one hundred percent of the time. It is also one hundred percent worth it.

One evening, I timidly went to Laurie about my wrestling with sexual temptation. Because we both have brokenness in the same area of sexual sin, she automatically abounds in compassion toward my problems with lust.

"I am about at an eight or nine on the struggle-with-sin-ometer," I said sheepishly. Scaling our temptation helps the other know how serious it is. A nine or ten means, "Keep me away from my computer and people who might tempt me." A three or four is usually where my struggle with lust hangs out. Somewhere in the middle requires a heart check.

Laurie didn't flinch.

She used to. Right after I came forward with my secret pornography addiction, she was afraid I would dive back in. Laurie learned to allow me to share my struggles in the moment by keeping her need for *protection* firmly fixed on God, not me.

When I told her I was high on the struggle-with-sin-ometer, simply seeing her react without fear helped to alleviate some of my struggle with lust. Sin grows in isolation and silence. Holiness grows in God-seeking community. She saw me in my mess and loved me, and I felt the number tick down a half of a point.

"What do you need?" she asked.

I looked inside, knowing she was asking about a Core Need. Of course, I wanted to be *desired*. It is my primary Core Need—the one that depletes the fastest. But which of my gardens needed its watering?

The casual, insensitive observer could step in and say, "You don't feel desired or wanted sexually by your wife. That's your problem, Matt. Tell her to get to it."

Telling Laurie to desire me wouldn't actually help me to see through her to God to meet this Core Need. I may feel physically desired but not at the level of our hearts. It would be a bodily act but not oneness. It would be similar to using pornography.

Additionally, if sex is a metaphor within the marriage metaphor of our present and future reality—our oneness with God— would God want us to mirror his love for us without our hearts involved? Never.

Am I ever going to demand Laurie's body without inviting her heart? No. It would damage her, hurt our marriage, and would no longer be engaging the kind of oneness God wants with us.

Instead of demand from her, I looked into other areas of my life where I might have felt a lack of desire. Family garden? No. Stewardship? No. What about the social garden? With Laurie, we had been interacting fine, but what about socializing with other people? There it is. I hadn't had bro time in weeks. "I think I need to call up the guys and watch a hockey game or something," I said. "I haven't had a chance to see them for a while."

"Go for it," she said with a smile. I know it's a sacrifice for her to take care of the kids on her own, but she knows it will fill me up.

So I watched a hockey game with some friends. We had no deep conversations, no "How's your heart?" moments—just a side-by-side acceptance and appreciation for each other.

In those spaces, barriers to my need to be *desired* can be removed. "I love you, Matt," I hear God say through my friends. "I desire to be with you. No pretense necessary. You don't have to try hard with me. We can just be together. Bro time." I don't often relate to the metaphor of God as my husband. My mind is too post-fall to understand the marriage reality we will experience in heaven. But Jesus as my older brother (Romans 8:29)? That I get. Through my friends' *desiring* to be with me, I feel he *desires* to be with me.

"How are you doing struggle-wise?" Laurie asked a few days later.

I peered inside my heart. "Huh, I'm at like a three or four now."

Nothing sexual happened. Nothing sexual needed to happen. But the need was met with brothers representing brother Jesus, and my struggle with lust was alleviated.

It's hard to live in this space—not diving into lust or detaching—it's hard to be in this awkward middle, vulnerable space. But it also feels right.

SEVEN

SO LONG, SHAME

When we are in the middle of a shame storm, it feels virtually impossible to turn again to see the face of someone, even someone we might otherwise feel safe with. It is as if our only refuge is in our isolation; the prospect of exposing what we feel activates our anticipation of further shame . . . It is in the movement toward another, toward connection with someone who is safe, that we come to know life and freedom from this prison.

CURT THOMPSON

LAURIE

I wanted to hide . . . again. I had been building muscles in my hands and arms as I held onto Jesus in the awkward middle, but I was triggered . . . again.

Matt tried to pursue me physically in the middle of the night. He was asleep, but his subconscious sought me out. When you have been traumatized, there is nothing more jarring than silent, physical pursuit while you sleep. The pursuer's silence paired with physical movement can mimic past assault. *What do you want? What are you doing? Do I have a choice?* You want to scream, but no words come out because your Broca's area in your brain has shut down just like when you were hurt.

All my fight-or-flight alarms set off until I pushed him away and I found my voice. "Go away. I'm tired." He did, but I did not feel empowered when I spoke. My words seemed to unlock the door to my familiar nemesis, toxic shame. It covered me in the sticky tar of self-contempt and lies.

Why can't you engage him physically like a "normal" wife? the shame spoke. *Other wives would be delighted that their kind, amazing, handsome husband wants to pursue them in the middle of the night.* I knew there was no way that was always true, but today it sounded like truth. *What's wrong with you?*

Toxic shame sounds like condemnation: *You are worthless.* It comes from the enemy, it's a whole-body feeling, and it happens before, during, or after we sin—or even if we don't sin! *You did what? You're worthless. You are tempted to do what? You're worthless. Sure, you confessed, but God still hates you. Worthless.*

Guilt or conviction on the other hand is sin-focused: *What you did was not worth it.* It's from the Lord. "Dear one, what you did right here—this specific thing—was not right. Confess that." It is a pinprick instead of a whole-body experience, and it only happens after we sin. It leads us to repentance. It leads to restored union with ourselves, the Father, and each other.

However, there is something else at play that helps us to feel the weight of our sin. I call it godly shame, and it reminds me of Paul's description of "godly sorrow [that] brings repentance" (2 Corinthians 7:10 NIV).[1] If guilt or conviction is the discovery of sin and confession of it, godly shame helps us to feel the weight of our sin contributing to the prevention of repeating the offense.

I understand that putting the word "shame" anywhere near the word "godly" feels so wrong—even to me! "Shred shame!" I have said many times. However, after studying it further, I do believe there is a godly version. Let me explain.

Paul utilizes godly shame in 1 Corinthians 6:5 when he writes, "I am saying this to shame you" to Christians who were suing each other in front of the watching world.[2] What kind of a witness is that? The world could therefore say, "You guys don't love each other? Neither do we. You fight nasty? So do we. Why do we want what you have?" The Corinthians needed to feel the weight of what they were doing, so Paul responded with godly shame. "This isn't right, church," he seemed to say. "Feel the conviction and confess. Feel the godly shame and work it out so that we do not continue in this path. People are watching. Your individual sin is affecting the whole, which is affecting our witness to the world that God loves them."

That is a big deal. If believers are doing things that cause the body to derail from our purpose of being one with the Father, one with each other, and inviting others into this oneness, they should feel godly shame.

We see Jesus use this type of shame as well. After his resurrection, he meets Peter again and they discuss his trifold failure of denying Jesus before his death. Jesus asks three times, "Peter, do you love me?" And three times Peter says, "You know that I love you." Then, Jesus invites him to feed his lambs (John 21:15-17).

What is happening here? How do we hear the kind of godly shame that helps us to feel the weight of what we did and prevents us from repeating the offense? Pastor and author Tim Keller captures it well:

> [Jesus] is recalling the denials. Three times He is saying, "Peter, you know you failed me." And every time, Peter is saying, "I know." "Peter, you know you failed me." . . . Peter says, "I know." That's not all that happens. Every time [Jesus] says, "You failed me," Peter does not get quiet, he does not say, "Why are you bringing this up again?" [and] he does not say, "I couldn't help it." Every time, Peter comes back and says, "Yeah, I know. But I still want to love you." . . . and Jesus says, "Now you are qualified."[3]

Jesus sounds like he is toxic shaming by bringing up past sin, but he isn't. Instead, he is embodying what love looks like in the midst of failure: "Dear one, you sinned. Confess it. Feel the weight of that sin so that you don't repeat it. You don't have to hate yourself because you fail. In fact, failing with me—if you stay with me—qualifies you for greater things."

I experienced this godly shame when I returned from the silent retreat, but I fought the toxic version. As I sat on the floor, looking at Matt's sad face, waiting for his forgiveness, I heard toxic shame: *You are worthless!* it spoke. "Nope," I spoke back. *Confess,* said conviction. I did. *Look at him,* said godly shame. I looked up. *His pain is right and good. You should feel remorse. Your sin isn't your own. It affects your marital unity, which affects church unity, which affects your witness to the world that God loves them. Don't do this again. Be one.*

Toxic shame is bathed in self-hatred. For too many years, I lived with it invading almost every thought. It has another name: the Accuser. And the Accuser has another name, Satan (Revelation 12:10).

He is good at making toxic shame sound like truth. When whispered at the right time—especially when you are alone—it seems like water to quench your battered soul.

You are worthless, he said.

Yes, I am, I agreed. *It is good for me to drink this in. I deserve it.*

After Matt's nighttime pursuit of me, I wrestled with talking to Matt about it. I fought the toxic shame and opened my mouth. "Do you remember last night . . .?" He didn't. He was sleeping. Matt hung his head low and sunk into his own bath of toxic, self-hating shame.

Toxic shame says, "You are worthless." Guilt, or conviction, speaks, "What you did was not worth it."

I hadn't sinned and neither had Matt, but here we were, both dripping in worthlessness.

Two points for Satan.

This was not the first time it had happened. Matt knew how triggering his silent, nighttime pursuit of me could be. He would put pillows between us as we slept and even offered to sleep in another room.

It was tempting, but I didn't truly want it. My will might have, but the spirit in me that wanted true oneness with him did not. If Matt gave up on our sexual relationship, it would be way easier for me to follow suit. I did not want the silent, middle-of-the-night interactions, but I also did not want Matt to quit on us. Stay in the awkward middle. Suffer well. Keep pursuing the marriage metaphor.

"No, don't do that," I said. "Just . . . try harder." That was the extent of our conversation as we were swept off into the day's work and kids and craziness with both.

But I carried the shame with me through it all. *I am worthless. I hate myself.*

I could almost hear the pendulum swinging back to isolation. Stepping in front of cars seemed tempting again.

But God never quits on us if we are willing to crack open our needy hearts even a fraction to him. He will dive into that space with all of himself (James 4:8).

This time, God used our children—the fruit of our oneness— to wake me up, pull me off the pendulum, and stick me back into the awkward middle.

Our now two-year-old, Juliette, was jumping on our bed while I got ready for our evening small group. I started playing "I'm a hungry crocodile," chasing her around the bed. She giggled, flopping onto the comforter.

I heard the door shut downstairs. *Matt is home.* A horrific familiar nudge poked at my heart: *I should go welcome him home . . . but I don't want to.* No! That was old Laurie. Old Laurie was the one who didn't want to be with Matt. The one who ran. The one who felt sadness at the Memory, fear from triggering, shame from the Accuser, and covered it all in a nice layer of anger. *That's not who I am anymore.* But I couldn't motivate myself to mechanically greet him. It felt too fake. Faking or detaching was an even older Laurie. *Help me, God.*

That prayer cracked open the door of my heart to hear God's voice instead of my shame alone.

God directed my eyes to my giggling daughter who was watching me, waiting for me to either go greet Dad or keep playing with her. *What will Mama do?*

I looked at Juliette and then I suddenly *saw* her. *She is fruit of oneness with Matt.* Then I saw her see me. *Our oneness is a witness to her.* Our oneness is a witness to our children that God wants to be one with them.

When I begin a discipleship relationship, I often ask about parents or caregivers. "How did your mom treat your dad? How did your dad treat your mom? How did they treat you?" Answers to these questions have a shockingly similarity to how we view God's treatment of us. "What comes into our minds when we think about God is the most important thing about us," theologian A. W. Tozer wrote.[4] Why would we look to God to care for our toxic shame-filled hearts if our image of him is a replication of our imperfect parents?

I had done enough soul work to at least catch myself when I was viewing God like my mom and dad, but I hadn't *really* thought that our kids will do the same thing with imperfect us. One day they will sit down with a therapist or mentor and hash out how we related to each other and them. Although we will inevitably fail at perfectly emulating a perfect God, we shouldn't quit trying. We need to ask the Lord to empower us to love our spouses with sacrificial love so that our oneness is a witness to our children that sacrificial God loves them.

Agony and conviction fought as my daughter looked into my eyes. *What will Mama do? Pursue Dad? Or play with me?*

The "right" answer in our kid-centric world seems like, "Keep playing with your child. Stare into her eyes. Tell her you see her. Meet those Core Needs." True, sometimes. It is critical for our children to have focused time with their parents, just as God has focused time with us.

But is it possible for our kids to feel more *delighted* in, *protected*, and *loved* when they see Mom and Dad loving each other well?

I thought of our oldest daughter, Gwyn, who, at four years old, asked Mom and Dad to "dance like a Disney movie." I am the first to point out the ways some of these films purport a false reality, but in other ways they don't. Certainly, they fall short of reality. The happily-ever-after endings of films like *Cinderella, Beauty and the Beast,* and *The Little Mermaid* point to human marriage as the ultimate answer to life's pain. But we know the marriage between Christ and the church is the true answer to life's pain. All of the needs of our hearts will one day be met in the new heavens and new earth.

So, when Gwyn asked Matt and me to dance, we looked at each other sheepishly and thought to ourselves, *Well, for the sake of the kid?* Our hands were unfamiliar with grasping one another, our hearts still shredded from painful conversations, our faces still drying from many tears. But we linked fingers and waltzed to a romantic song rotating on the family playlist. For a minute, our bodies synchronized, as well as our hearts. *Oh, yeah . . . you. There's something intangibly connecting us, isn't there? Someone bigger than us wants us together.*

When we looked at Gwyn, we were shocked at her four-year-old reaction. She clasped her hands together, tipped her head sideways, and smiled with a sigh. You could see what our oneness did to her heart. She felt *protected. Loved. Delighted* in. And we weren't staring at her. We were staring at each other. But she seemed to see through us to . . . something. A longing in her own self. In that moment, I could have said as I saw that longing, "Someday, honey! Someday you will find a man to dance with, and he will meet all of your heart needs." But I know that is a lie. Instead, I needed to say and model, "Gwyn, when you see your dad and me love each other well, we are showing you how much God loves you."

That desire for oneness with God should make us all clasp our hands, tip our heads to the side, and smile-sigh with a deep, longing hope.

Back in our bedroom, as Juliette waited to see if I would continue as a crocodile or welcome her dad home, God seemed to whisper to me, *Include Juliette in your oneness now. Include her*

*in the love dance you know you can have with Matt because I am the
one who is writing the music that synchronizes you.*

I gritted my teeth. To do that in this freshly triggered state—
not in a mechanical, detached, old Laurie way—I needed to dig
through the layers I had piled on since the incident. Not only did
I have toxic shame to deal with, but I had covered it all day in
anger toward Matt (*He should know better!*) and toward myself
(*I am the worst wife. Why is he with me?*).

Psychologist Dan Allender says this self-and-others contempt
is a common go-to for those of us who deal with shame.

> Contempt is our way to manage shame with a level of
> control that annihilates ourselves so that we don't
> feel. . . . Whether it's self-contempt . . . or other-centered
> contempt, in either form it's the same brick but directed in
> a very different direction. It ultimately lessens our sense of
> shame but in the long run, it only intensifies it.[5]

Instead of feeling the ambiguous shame, we try to control it by
gripping an easier emotion, like anger. We turn the knife inward or
chuck it at the world. I had chosen both, but I did not have to
choose either of them. I picked up the blade and started hacking at
the true enemy—toxic shame. The Accuser. Satan. My anger became
a tool I could use to tear through that second layer of shame.

*No. Back off. I am a child of the King. You may not lie to me anymore.
I am not worthless. I am healing. I am not a freak. I am in-process.*
Whatever Core Need felt empty in me, I started speaking life into,
even if I didn't feel it. *I am beloved. I am chosen. God delights in me.*

Then, I moved on to fear of Matt.

Little Laurie is scared of Matt, I thought. *Not the adult. I am no
longer a child. I am an adult. I get to choose. I choose Matt.*

The fear didn't grip me as hard in the middle of this shower
of truth.

What about sadness? Well . . . I was still sad about the pain of
the Memory. But sadness—although more vulnerable than
anger-shame—can invite oneness.

True grief opens up our hearts to God and people. Anger-shame wedges us apart. Sadness could stay.

My daughter was still waiting.

I smiled at her. "Okay, little crocodile. Daddy's home. Let's go welcome him." She giggled as I scooped her into my arms. She was completely unaware of how these tiny moments of her parents pursuing each other were forming her perception of God, as well as the battle it took for us to get there.

But my Father knew. And as we as we marched down the stairs, I could feel an extra squeeze in my still-sad-but-not-angry-or-toxin-laden heart. God saw me. He knew the fight no one else knew. And he was proud.

• • •

MATT

When I was addicted to pornography, toxic shame was my closest friend.

When I felt empty, unloved, unwanted, I turned to porn to fill me up. I didn't often intentionally plan my life around it, but some days I did. *Laurie is gone tonight, so . . .* My brain said, "I feel empty, therefore, porn will satisfy me." This is an illogical thought that makes me shake my head now. But when we are alone and lonely, our Core Needs exposed and empty, the illogical becomes logical. Lies sound like truth.

Most evenings after Laurie went to bed, I unintentionally wandered there. I was like the fool in Proverbs who wandered near the door of the adulterous woman (Proverbs 5:7-9). *Maybe something will happen? Maybe it won't?* But deep down, I wanted it to because lies had become truth. *If I wander, I will become full.*

Porn knocks on the door of your ravaged heart, promises to meet all of your needs to be *desired, noticed*, and made whole. But after you engage, it leaves you feeling worse than before and needing more.

Toxic shame meets you there with open arms.

You are worthless, Matt, it said.

Yes. I am, I believed. *It's good for me to drink this in. I deserve it.* Toxic shame (a.k.a. the Accuser) took those needs that felt temporarily met with porn and kicked them. When I felt horrible about myself, I confessed to God, "I'm so sorry. I'll do better tomorrow." But I didn't. I couldn't. Behavioral modification only lasts so long when your heart is full of weeds.

I needed living water to heal me, but I was drinking pebbles. I wasn't even drinking bad water; I was sucking down something that wasn't even liquid—tiny rocks I pretended were delicious and satisfying.

I was sitting in my need to be *desired,* away from the source of living water, and I invited digital strangers to cultivate that space. It was my separate life. My new dead garden, the one that held my favorite Core Need in my favorite physical garden.

But any life we create outside of God's design only brings death. Barriers built up between my need to be *desired* and finding fulfillment in God. Weeds hid me from my co-gardener. As a result, all of my gardens started dying.

"Matt? Are you there?" Laurie would ask from the emotional or social garden.

"Yeah! Totally! I'm here!" I yelled. My voice carried, but I couldn't go there. I was stuck now in my favorite garden with my favorite Core Need, a slave to what I thought promised freedom (2 Peter 2:19).

When I finally realized my self-deceit, I confessed. But I didn't let godly shame and conviction bring me to true repentance. I confessed and let toxic shame beat me.

That was my life. Fall, get kicked, confess, fall, get kicked, confess . . .

Periods of days or weeks would come where I walked in some semblance of freedom, but then . . . life. I had a high-pressure job where I was not very gifted, and I felt like a total failure. My Core Needs felt empty, and I fell into hiding.

Porn promised I wouldn't feel like a failure. I could be a king . . . for a few minutes.

And then there was Laurie. All of this happened years before her confrontation with the Memory, and she was often kind, gracious, and giving—far more than I deserved.

I did not always reciprocate. I was never abusive or overly harsh, but porn messes with your ability to choose kindness and genuine love. During sexual intimacy in marriage, both parties feel the happy high of dopamine, the bonding of oxytocin, the mood stabilization of serotonin, and the remembering agent of norepinephrine. God brilliantly designed hormones to help us bond with our spouse. However, we also get the high of these hormones if physically stimulated while watching pornography. We can bond to a computer. To a screen. But we weren't made to bond to a screen *and* a spouse. We are made for intimacy with one person, and if we choose the screen over our spouse, we automatically create an outgroup. That outgroup is our spouse and our kids. We can become aggressive toward them because they are keeping us from that to which we are bonded.[6]

That happened to me. I never became violent or even loud, but I was short-tempered and picked fights over inane things. I will never forget a wake-up call I had after hanging out with Laurie's sister and brother-in-law. For some reason, I got stuck on Laurie making coffee in the afternoon. I was so mad that she was wasting the coffee instead of simply taking a nap. Understandably, she did not want to take a nap, as it would limit the already limited time she had with her sister. I see the logic now, but then? I was relentless.

"Why are you making coffee for a second time today?" I asked rudely. "Just take a nap." Instead of fighting back, she shut down. Our guests tiptoed around us and our unnecessary argument. Minutes after the door closed on their exit, Laurie looked me in the eye and respectfully and honestly said, "You know my sister is afraid of you, right?" I was shocked. *How could that be? I'm the nicest guy.* I was known as *the* nice guy in high school and college. *When did I get so angry?*

But instead of connecting my anger to my pornography use, to cover the shame even of this moment, I went back to pornography use. To solve the issues created by drinking toilet water, I went back to that very same toilet water.

I didn't know how to find freedom.

Curt Thompson, in his book *The Soul of Shame,* describes how when we feel a sense of worthlessness over what we are doing, we think hiding is the right option.

> When we are in the middle of a shame storm, it feels virtually impossible to turn again to see the face of someone, even someone we might otherwise feel safe with. It is as if our only refuge is in our isolation; the prospect of exposing what we feel activates our anticipation of further shame.[7]

Hiding because of toxic shame begets hiding because of toxic shame.

Adam and Eve did this. They felt shame over their sin and hid. But what is so interesting to me is that even though they sinned by eating the fruit from the forbidden tree, their whole bodies were cringing. "I heard you walking in the garden, so I hid," Adam said to God. "I was afraid because I was naked" (Genesis 3:10). Wait . . . why are they ashamed at their nakedness? Just a few verses earlier, they were naked and free, feeling "no shame" (2:25).

What's going on? Right here, at the first sin, we see Satan attach a feeling of worthlessness to sin. Adam and Eve hid because of nakedness, but nakedness wasn't the sin. They felt ashamed. But what kind of shame? Godly or toxic? Godly shame is a red-faced feeling that fuels in us an understanding that what we did wasn't worth it. It says, "I broke union between myself and God, between myself and believers. I contributed to making our mission to make disciples more challenging. I want to repent to get back to oneness with God and believers." We need to feel this godly shame.

When Adam and Eve sinned, they broke union with the Father and changed the course of history. They should have felt some red-faced, godly shame about it. However, they could have just as easily hid because of toxic shame: "We sinned and are worthless. Run from God!" Only God knows which reasoning inspired their decision to hide. Likely it was a combination of both, but thankfully the solution for both is the same thing: God's pursuit in the stormy mess of shame.

"Where are you?" God called (3:9). Curt Thompson adds depth to this scene by observing, "It is in the *movement toward another*, toward connection with someone who is safe, that we come to know life and freedom from this [shame storm] prison."[8] When we are seen and loved in our mess, God can remove toxic shame from our messy situation. When toxic shame is removed, we can repent and come back into union with him and the body of Christ.

Adam and Eve came out of hiding and said they had hidden because of their nakedness. "Who told you that you were naked?" God asked (3:11). I have often read this verse in an angry-God voice, but I wonder if his question was laced with sadness instead. Instead of shaming their shame, he cares for them. He makes clothes for them (3:21). But he doesn't downplay the gravity of their actions or remove their godly shame and guilt.

That's how God operated with me. He pursued me in my mess and removed toxic shame from my messy situation, but he left me with godly shame and good guilt. And he used my wife to bring me there.

I was terrified to come forward to Laurie. I told myself it was because I was the one man she trusted. She was wrestling through bitterness toward most men who she generally viewed as being run by their sex drives. I didn't want to be categorized with "bad men." I wanted to be in the "good men" group. I liked when she told me, "You are so honorable, Matt. I am so glad I can trust you." Even though I cringed inside because it wasn't true, her words felt like a paradise island as I swam in sewer water.

I will take this to my grave, I said of pornography. *She will leave me if I tell her.*

So, I kept sitting in my favorite physical garden with my favorite need to be *desired* and ate pebbles.

But as I did, I noticed my growing anger at others. I became depressed.

Someone once called depression "frozen rage." That was true of my depression in that season. Sometimes my rage thawed and washed over Laurie, but most of it focused inward. I covered my Core Needs with sadness, covered sadness with sin, and covered sin with contempt for others and self.

A good friend who knew nothing of my porn addiction connected me to a counselor to help with my depression. I didn't want to go, afraid that this counselor might see more than I wanted her to. She was known for prophetic, truth-telling words, and I thought she might peer into my soul with the Holy Spirit and convict me like the prophet Nathan did to the adulterer King David (2 Samuel 12:5-7).

Instead of pointing the finger at me, though, this counselor brought me to a place of prayer where I saw more than the backs of my eyelids. It was my first real experience with visual prayer. I didn't know if it was theologically permissible, but I was so desperate for living water that I was willing to try.[9] Since that first experience, I have learned to see visual prayer from the perspective of theologian R. A. Torrey: "We should never utter one syllable of prayer either in public or in private, until we are definitely conscious that we have come into the presence of God, and are actually praying to Him."[10] Torrey goes so far as to say that praying without recognizing who we are speaking to is the same as taking God's name in vain.

I didn't know what would happen when I shut my eyes, but as we prayed, the Holy Spirit brought to mind a picture of myself as a young boy with a bulging backpack full of burdens and pain. I dragged it up to the top of a hill next to a lonely tree.

"I can't do it!" I yelled up toward God from the peak of the hill. I was in Little Matt's body, but I had Adult Matt's understanding. "I can't carry this load by myself. I am so overwhelmed by my own ineptitude. I am failing at my job. Failing with my wife. I am a failure . . ."

The scene shifted from lonely, overwhelmed, little-boy me yelling at the sky to Jesus joining me. My yelling stopped in the presence of his understanding smile. He put a strong and tender hand on my shoulder and the backpack of my burdens fell off. I felt enormous relief. *I don't have to carry it!* Jesus took his hands from my shoulders and pulled me into a welcome embrace. His arms spoke silent love from my skin to my bones. To my soul. To me. He *knew* me. And yet he loved me.

Jesus pulled back and looked into my eyes. "Know that you are loved, Matt." This was interesting phrasing. He didn't say, "I love you." He said, "*Know* it." As in, believe it. Stop hiding and start believing you have worth because *I love you.* But you must choose to believe it.

As I walked down the hill in this prayerful place, I was no longer Little Matt but Adult Matt who knew he was loved.

That love empowered me to face Laurie one month later.

She was attending a small group led by the same counselor who guided me in prayer. The other women in the group lived like they believed we fight more than flesh and blood enemies. They prayed in faith and challenged each other to live like Christ. Laurie was clearly growing. She prayed bolder prayers and believed she had a calling on her life. She was becoming a warrior — a warrior woman who *knew* she was loved.

One night, Laurie got up to help our six-month-old baby who had cried out in the night. When she tried to settle back down to sleep, Laurie sensed a darkness in the air. With faith, she began praying over our house for protection. After several minutes, she woke me up to ask me to help. "Do your manly duty," she said with a tinge of joking and fear. "I can't seem to get this darkness out on my own. You are the head of the house, so please help."

Oh, man. I thought. *I don't know how to do this.* Laurie could run circles around me spiritually. I was still working on getting the ABCs down of knowing I was loved. I had already fallen several times with pornography since encountering Jesus. *God, help me. Who am I to pray?* If courage is moving through your fear, I stepped into courage and prayed. "God, let there be no spirit in this house that is not of you." That sentence flew out of my mouth like an arrow and came back into my heart.

It's you, Matt. You are the one inviting these evil spirits into this house.

I was shaken. After a few minutes, Laurie said she sensed it had lifted. "Not totally, but somewhat." This way she viewed the spiritual world as something real was so new to me—and her. But I knew what she was seeing was true. *It's me. I am inviting evil into this house.*

I'll try harder, God, I pleaded as I tried to fall asleep. *I will know I am loved, and I won't do it again.*

No, Matt. I heard his voice calm and true. *You need to tell the one you have wronged.*

Laurie. God wanted me to tell Laurie. God wanted me to shred shame by being seen by someone in my mess. *No! How about someone else? A friend? An accountability partner? She'll hate me! Leave me! I have nothing other than how she views me.*

I will not bless you until you tell the one you have wronged, he said.

Fine! I looked over at her. I often take hours to fall back asleep if I wake up at night, but Laurie has a superpower to drift to dreamland in seconds. *Fine . . . if she wakes up right now.* I knew she wouldn't. She falls asleep quickly and only the cries of our children can wake her up.

I turned over, ready to snuggle in for the night, but my arm leapt from my side as if it had its own mind and thwapped Laurie awake.

"What?" she said groggily. I glared upward at God and then slowly unfolded the truth to Laurie about my secret addiction for six years of our marriage.

This was the beginning of my season of repentance. I had accepted Christ as a kid, but this moment was when I truly came to know him—mostly through the grace Laurie showed me. She did not reject me like I thought she would. She was hurt. Sad. Righteously angry. She considered leaving for two seconds, but when she saw how her sexual struggles were the same as mine, she was able to extend empathy. When she helped me uncover the true need below my sinful desires, she became my closest friend again.[11]

Her seeing me in my mess and loving me helped me to shred my old nemesis, toxic shame.

Know you are loved.

But here we were, a couple of years later, and Laurie hung out with toxic shame so often. I wanted to see her in her mess and love her as she was, thereby removing the power of shame from her like God did with me—but she cowered from me.

I knew she was all in our marriage. I knew she had chosen me. I knew she was growing in her theology of oneness.

But the Memory locked her up, gripped her sexual orientation, and paved an easy pathway for shame to relentlessly assault her day after day.

You are worthless.

You will never be healed.

You're stuck.

Your marriage is doomed.

It was time to go to war.

EIGHT

WARRIORS

Lament is one of the most direct paths to the true praise we know
we have lost. In fact, lament is not a path to worship, but the path
of worship.... Once tasted, this praise leaves every other pretended
praise tasteless. It issues forth from the rubble of a once holy city.
It can only come from the fragmented ruins of a once whole life.
It can only echo from the wilderness.

MICHAEL CARD

LAURIE

I was absolutely desperate: *God, where is the miracle for me? I'll*
swim in the dirty waters of the Jordan. Let your spit restore me.
Please, let me touch your robe so that I can be healed.[1]

I kept waiting to discover the right combination to unlock
God's breakthrough: counseling, marriage intensives, books on
trauma, praying with close friends, visual prayer with the woman
who had led me through other trauma processing, praying with
Matt, praying alone, praying with pastors ... was this my lot in
life? Was there nothing that would help?

I was fine with the attractions toward women. They were no
longer the enticing escape they had been the year before on the
silent retreat. They were, and likely will, always be present until
I see Jesus someday, but they didn't *own* me. They were present
but not powerful. And if they became powerful again? I knew the
right path was to pursue Core Needs instead of sexual wants.

I was mostly fine with having no physical relationship with my husband—although I was glad to be somewhat not-fine with it. That showed growth. I desired for Matt—not all men, but Matt—to see through me to God who wants to be one with him holistically. I wanted to kick Satan in the teeth by being close to Matt physically. I wanted our oneness to be a witness to the world that said our marriage was impossible. "Yes!" we could say. "It is without Christ, but so is yours. So is all of our marriage to the One. Our marriage to God is only made possible because of Jesus Christ."

Where I was *not fine* was walking any longer with the Memory. I was sick of it sitting like a boulder in our physical garden. It felt like it was getting worse—maybe growing a fungus that was spreading to all of the other gardens.

Won't you heal me, God?

I was willing to give it one more try. I had tried to go back to the time of the Memory several times in therapy and visual prayer. During each attempt, I either shifted into some sort of catatonic state, my image went completely black or red, or I was so triggered that I couldn't recover for hours or days.

It made no sense to me. I had processed three other traumatic memories from my past with a combination of talk therapy and visual prayer *and it had worked every time*. These memories didn't disappear as if they had never happened, but love transformed them. When I was eight and my ballet teacher touched me inappropriately? I saw God show up—righteously angry. When I was nine and a family friend played a game with me that wasn't a game? God appeared as my defender. When I was assaulted by a stranger in a store in the toy aisle at the age of eleven? Jesus showed me he hadn't sent the man to hurt me. He was there with me when it happened with his hand on my back, weeping.

Where are you now?

Because of what I was learning about God and the ways I was growing, I tried to get closer to Matt physically—but every time I did, my entire body slammed into the Memory. I collapsed inside, literally curled up into the fetal position, dropped my sleep mask over my eyes, and drifted into dreamless sleep.

"Every time I am triggered like that, I feel like I die," I said to Matt. "But the deaths don't start fresh the next day. They compound. The fungus-like memory takes over more of my body." I started feeling physical pain inside. "There is no way this is God's will for me."

Maybe now is the time. Maybe now I am strong enough. All of my studying of a better theology of marriage, shedding toxic shame, learning that I am *Adult* Laurie and not a child—it had led me to this moment.

Maybe now is the time.

So, I put on my armor and we went to war.[2]

I fasted that day and texted friends to pray. "Tonight, after we record the podcast, Matt and I are going to try to go back to the Memory through visual prayer. Please pray."

I knew I might get retriggered and internally die again, but it couldn't be worse than dragging death around in my chest every day. I was willing to try.

Our kids were sleeping when we got home from recording. It was another good interview. Our guest, Branson Parler, caused Matt and me to look up from our pain and see each other. *Oh, yeah . . . you. Oneness.* Branson not only spoke about marriage and singleness with such reverence that I wanted to worship God while recording, he talked about how the tangible nature of sex represents our tangible God. "Our bodies matter. Matter matters," he said. "The way God communicates his love to us is not just through this intellectual message that bounces off of us—the Word became flesh."[3] When we have sex with our spouse, we image Jesus' tangible pursuit of oneness with us.

I took this discussion as a sign that the time was now. *Please, God. Could you please take away this chronic pain of my soul? Then maybe Matt and I will have the holistic marriage we are supposed to have. Please, Jesus?*

We sat in our matching 1970s light blue armchairs, and Matt began praying. The way we have been trained to do visual prayer is to begin with what is called a "safe place" when we know we are going to go back to a place of trauma.[4] Beginning and ending in a place where we feel safe helps decrease the triggering or detachment that can occur when plainly talking about trauma.

After a moment, God brought me to my usual safe place. It was that field by the pond behind one of my family houses—where Little Matt had joined me to play with kittens. I saw the reeds dancing in the breeze, and Jesus seemed to be there. At least, he looked like Jesus, but he didn't act like the one I knew. He was repelled by me, like two opposite parts of a magnet. Then I saw another Jesus walking around. And another and another. The atmosphere became noisy, dark, frightening, like a bomb had just detonated. The sky turned pink and grey and hazy—terrifying and without a lick of safety.

This isn't right. The enemy is interfering, I thought.

Doing this practice hundreds of times with ourselves and others has taught us to always keep the Bible over our eyes, ears, and mouths. As Tim Keller says, "Without prayer that answers the God of the Bible, we will only be talking to ourselves."[5] In that moment, I didn't want to talk to myself. I needed real God, so I told Matt what I was seeing. He recognized that confusing, terrifying place would not be a product of God who is a God of peace and order (1 Corinthians 14:33). "Do you need to go to another safe place?" Matt asked. Yes. I did. In my mind, I lit the place on fire and walked away like the end of good action movie.

"God, will you please take me somewhere else that is actually safe?" I prayed.

I immediately saw a familiar beach. I'd been to this part of Lake Michigan's shore many times before but only once when it looked like this—chilly, the sun setting, and completely empty. It was after I returned from studying abroad at Oxford University, and I was so doubly hungry for the beach and for an encounter with God that I had driven over a hundred miles per hour to get there. I felt the same hunger but thankfully did not need to make a dangerous decision to get there. I could close my eyes and return immediately.

I looked down at my feet buried in the chilly sand. I could feel remnants of the day's sunshine the deeper I dug. I drank in the view of the orange-pink sunset and listened to the waves lap on the lonely shore. I glanced to my left and saw Jesus next to me. He buried his feet, too, and smiled at me. Knowing me. Getting me.

"Can you talk to him?" Matt asked, gently weaving his narrative voice through the scene. I nodded, my eyes still closed. "Is he close to you?"

I nodded again. "Right beside me but not touching me."

It's always interesting to me to note where God physically is in these prayerful spaces. Is he close? Is he far? How do I feel about him putting his arm around me? Do I want him to? How I "see" him in these spaces is often reflective of how I am experiencing his intimacy in real life.

"Do you want to talk with him?" Matt asked. I did.

The tears began immediately. Jesus does that to me. "It hurts," I cried. "It's too much." Of course, I was talking about the Memory, but he knew that.

Matt asked if I could tell how Jesus felt about me. I looked into his eyes—laugh lines surrounding them. *He gets me.* "I'm not too much for him," I said. Jesus' eyes didn't flicker with the uncertainty and fear I had seen from other people so many times over the last two years. The look they gave me when I shared pieces of our real lives communicated, "Oh, shoot. What do I do with her? Same-sex attractions *and* trauma? *And* she is in ministry? *And* she can't have sex with her husband? Hot. Mess." But Jesus was confident. He wasn't afraid of me. Image bearers are never too much for the image, Jesus.

Suddenly we were flying over the water. I wasn't scared or surprised. I knew where we were going.

We landed in the bathroom where the trauma had happened, but the time was different. The trauma had happened in the morning, but now it was late afternoon. This is my favorite time of day, because the sun cuts sideways through windows and casts beautiful oblong shapes on the ground. As a child, I loved to lay in the shadows and daydream about the future.

But now I wasn't sitting in the pretty shapes on the bathroom floor. I was both in an empty bathtub and in three-year-old Laurie's body.

"How does Laurie feel in that empty tub?" Matt asked.

I felt inside the emotional world of my little-girl self. "She is confused as to why she is still here. The bath is over. The trauma is done, but it's like she's stuck. She can't leave."

It reminded me of what a friend had said the day before. "Laurie, it seems like you can't get freedom because you are stuck wherever that memory occurred." She was right—but now I could *see* it.

Little Laurie wanted to understand why she was stuck. *What happened to me?* I asked.

The time changed to the morning it happened. I looked down again at my little-girl legs and they were covered in water. This was familiar to me. I had seen pieces of this scene before when I had gone back through prayer or in talk therapy. I felt my real heart racing, waiting for my brain to shut down.

But it didn't. I stayed as little-girl Laurie but felt more grounded this time. Grounded in theology. Grounded in knowing, *I am not her. I am an adult.* Grounded in prayer. Grounded as Matt—the one I almost left, largely because of this memory—led me in this visual prayer.

I'm okay even though she's not okay. The scene got noisier. Splashy. Uncomfortable. Blurry and loud. I knew there was a person watching me . . . or touching me? He was a stranger. I *knew* he was a stranger.

I wanted to know the details. *Is this someone who was working on our house? A builder? Painter?* We had recently moved into this new home. *Why is he here?* But a quiet voice told me I didn't need to know. I didn't need to know the details. I just needed to know something happened.

But that lack of knowing started a wave of fear in me that I couldn't shake. I began to panic, breathing quickly. Matt asked me questions, but my mouth couldn't move. I froze next to him in the armchair. My arms and legs felt numb. Adult Laurie and Little Laurie silently screamed inside—begging for a rescuer. *Is someone here who can save me?!*

Jesus. He stepped in to break the bond forming between me and the man in the Memory. *Is this man touching me? Looking at me? Is he even real? Why can't I see him?* Jesus' courage reached out to me like a calm wave. *Jesus is inviting me to do something. But isn't his strength enough?*

Matt's voice cut through the chaos. "Can you speak?" he asked. I opened my real-life mouth and tried to make a sound. I could. A lightbulb went off somewhere in my mind. *Oh! Jesus wants me to partner with him to remove this man. He wants me to see I have strength because of his strength in me. I have a voice.* I used it. "Get away from me." It was so quiet. Flat. No inflection. "Go. Get away. I don't want you." They were small sentences—nothing extraordinarily powerful—just the simple phrases of a three-year-old.

But each childish sentence compounded, adding strength to my soul. "Get away!" A little louder this time. "Get away from me!" He moved an inch, but that inch gave me a better picture of what was happening—not physically but spiritually. It wasn't just the man hurting me. Behind and beside him, I could see shoulder-to-shoulder evil. The room was thick with darkness.

The enemy wanted to destroy me at a young age. He wants to destroy all of us, at any age.

"No!" I said. "You can't have me. Get. Away."

Jesus empowered me to push the darkness back. A few inches now, but we needed something more.

"God, help!" Matt prayed, sensing the need. As he spoke, I saw myself grow older. I stood up from the tub. My once-frozen arms and legs could move and they grew with rippling muscles as I flexed them. I saw I was at least eight-feet tall and well-used armor covered my body. I was no longer Little Laurie. I wasn't even busted up Adult Laurie. I was Wonder Woman Laurie. Warrior Laurie.

The Holy Spirit also joined the fight, like a bright, raging, holy wind.

I sensed the Spirit whisper that we needed more help. *Who?* I asked. *You're God! Aren't you enough?* Of course, God is enough, but he is about our sanctification. We can only become like him by getting in the battle. *I'm already in. Who else can join?* Matt, of course.

He's a warrior too, the Holy Spirit whispered.

"Matt, can you pray?" I asked desperately. He was praying for me already but not with me. Not next to me. "Can you help me fight this evil?" He paused, thinking. This strange visual prayer space was new and somewhat scary for him. But he knew it was for me too. "Okay," he said, determined and brave. "God, help. Help, Jesus!" I knew he could at least vaguely see what I could see. I didn't need to describe it. He was no longer the narrator but an armor-clad, eight-foot warrior beside me.

Together, praying in the power of the Spirit, the darkness backed up twice as quickly. Within minutes, all of the darkness was gone. It fled. It had to.

We breathed heavily as if we had just run a marathon. Jesus walked through the dust, and the time shifted into late afternoon again—a safe, nonthreatening time of day. *Jesus is so kind. So thoughtful.*

I could tell he was proud of us but not overly impressed. This wasn't because we did not do well but because I could tell he thought that *this should be normal.* Normal warfare. Normal battle. We did great, but we hadn't vanquished sin and death forever. He would do that later. This battle seemed so big and horrific to me, but the sense I got from Jesus' lack of enthusiasm was that these sorts of skirmishes should happen often.

I smiled at Matt in the now darkness-free bathroom. If this was normal, there would be more battles together. More battles for our freedom, our children's liberty, and that of other warrior-saints who are stuck.

Wonder Woman Laurie looked over at the bathtub. I was surprised to see Little Laurie there again. Her soul was still there. *Why? Didn't we just vanquish the Memory? Didn't we just show Little Laurie who really wins?*

"Can you go to her?" Matt asked. "Can you comfort her? Tell her she is going to be okay?"

My armor clinked as I walked over. I could tell she still felt confused and scared but somewhat more confident. She knew a battle had happened. The evil was gone, but she was paralyzed. Stuck.

I bent down and reached out to her. This seemed to wake her up from her stupor, and she quickly wrapped her arms around my neck. I held her close, comforting her. I no longer resented this Little Laurie who interrupted my life. I ached for her. *I'm so sorry I hated you.*

She gripped me tightly, forgiving me.

"It's going to be okay," I said. "You're safe now. I'm here. We are all here." I indicated to Matt and Jesus.

Matt had tears streaming down his face.

Jesus drew close. He knew what Little Laurie needed and held out the softest, fluffiest, sparkling white robes. I set her down, and he crouched to wrap her shivering body in the snuggly clothes.

He hugged her close—the safest touch from God-man to this beloved little girl. Nothing like what I had endured from the evil. Jesus smiled, stood up, and offered his hand to her. *He always offers, never demands.* She looked up at his face and trusted, placing her hand in his. As they walked, they talked quietly together. I couldn't hear everything but did overhear this: "I'm going to use this, dear one." She didn't understand, but I did. I knew he was thinking of all the trauma I would endure even after this one. He would transform all of those moments to show her more of his love in suffering.

When Jesus and Little Laurie reached the door, they stopped and turned toward Matt and me. I was still sweaty, bloody from the fight, tears dripping down my face cutting through the grime. Matt looked similar. Jesus pointed at me and whispered into Little Laurie's ear, "You are going to be her someday."

Her eyes went wide, her jaw dropped, and she turned to Jesus. "What? Really?" She giggled, dumbfounded at the idea. Clearly, she thought Warrior Laurie was too amazing to be connected to her little self.

"Yeah!" Jesus said excitedly. "You are!"

Little Laurie chuckled again and gave me a thumbs up. I did the same to her.

Yeah, I thought as we smiled at each other. *You will become me one day, but it is because of the pain. It is because of the trauma. It is because you do not give up in suffering that you can become this strong.*

I ached for her while I hoped for her.

I wonder if this is how Jesus feels for all of us all of the time: aching, hoping, helping.

I waved at Little Laurie as she and Jesus turned to leave. I knew she was going back to live her life, but it didn't seem like the same life anymore. Life is a training school for spiritual battles.

I opened my real eyes and looked at Matt anew. He was still a warrior, just without the armor.

"When did we forget we were co-warriors?" he asked. I didn't know. Sometime over the last year. "Let's not forget again, okay?"

I nodded. Never again. Not just because we are Christians who stay married because we're "supposed to" but because we need each other to fight the real enemy.

With a small gasp, I remembered the reason we had engaged in this visual prayer in the first place. I searched inside, waiting to bump into the boulder of the Memory. I didn't feel it. I still remembered it—even more clearly now—but it was transformed during the battle.

God smashed the rock into seeds. This sort of death-to-life transformation is his specialty (Isaiah 61:1-7).

I did not know what type of tree would grow from this suffering, but I knew it would be strong. The heartiest trees grow in the most brutal conditions.

What I had thought was impossible—the transformation of the Memory—was made possible with Jesus Christ.

"I think I'm free," I said to Matt. He smiled and gently squeezed my hand. "I can't believe it. After years of being stuck, I'm free."

• • •

MATT

Praying with Laurie through this memory pushed me out of my comfort zone.

Before I surrendered my own version of broken sexuality to Jesus, almost everything spiritually related beyond going to church and praying before meals was outside of my comfort zone.

Sometimes, I would engage in a lighter version of this kind of prayer because the Spirit inside of me gave me a hunger for more than my toxic shame and self-hatred.

Mostly, I avoided. I must have been too tired to fight the Spirit the night I accidentally prayed the prayer that led to freedom from pornography.

I am so glad I was too tired.

Since that transforming prayer, I pushed myself to more frequently engage in challenging spiritual spaces (the spiritual garden). I want to experience all that God had to offer.

Many men miss out on this. Some of us are not trained to pursue this space. We are told to buck up and fix problems, or our dads showed us a form of masculinity that avoids anything intangible, like emotions. But what most of us don't want to admit that it isn't our faith in God that keeps us from engaging those spiritual spaces—it's our fear. We feel inadequate, something we were trained to never feel. So, we avoid it to keep from looking stupid.

In doing so, we miss out.

These places push me out of my head and into the Spirit where I have come to experience more of God's intense and personal love.

God is real, and he truly wants a relationship with us.

Prayer—specifically lament—is a way to connect to this real, relational God.

Lament is "a prayer for help coming out of pain," or, as Laurie and I say, lament is openhearted venting to someone who can do something about it.[6]

The visual prayer with which we'd engaged the Memory was a form of lament. Laurie took that pain and directed it at God. "Help me. This is on you to resurrect this dead place in me."

As a therapist, I am pro-holistic care. Cognitive behavioral therapy (CBT) can be a great technique for teaching coping skills to people with mental health issues. Practices like EMDR, narrative therapy, and mindfulness are extremely helpful for people with trauma in their past. Exercise, medications, and healthy eating also contribute to the care of a person's physical, mental, and emotional health.

But prayer contributes too. A study by researchers at Baylor University found that people with anxiety-related disorders who pray to a God they perceived as loving and protective experience less anxiety.[7] But only those who were able to perceive God as loving and protective. How do we see him that way? Can we shut our eyes and construct a nice, easygoing, hipster Jesus who is chill about everything—and still the protective Alpha and Omega?

No. Before we close our eyes and visualize him both as loving and a place of safety, we need to teach our imaginations how to see him this way by reading the Bible. We need to train our brains to know how he is loving and safe. He is not anything-goes loving. The biblical definition of love includes rejoicing "whenever the truth wins out" (1 Corinthians 13:6). But neither is he impulsively vengeful. Just look at the narrative of the Old and New Testament! The Israelites—his people—failed over and over again and yet, "The LORD is compassionate and merciful, slow to get angry and filled with unfailing love" (Psalm 103:8).

Laurie could not have experienced the true God in that bathroom—righting the memory in the way he had—if she did not know what he was like. She learned his real character through years of shaping her understanding of God through the Word of God.

How does God feel about those who sin against little children? He cares deeply.

> If you cause one of these little ones who trusts in me to fall into sin, it would be better for you to have a large millstone tied around your neck and be drowned in the depths of the sea. . . . Beware that you don't look down on any of these little ones. For I tell you that in heaven their angels are always in the presence of my heavenly Father. (Matthew 18:6, 10)

How does God confront the most frightening things—literal, actual demons? He doesn't freak out. He doesn't have to shout. He confidently disarms them.

"Many were possessed by demons; and the demons came out at his command, shouting, 'You are the Son of God!' But because they knew he was the Messiah, he rebuked them and refused to let them speak" (Luke 4:41).[8]

How does he feel about sexual sinners?

He engages them and seems to go out of his way for them, as he did with the Samaritan woman at the well who had five husbands and was living with a man who was not her husband (John 4:4, 7).

What does God want us to do with our darkest emotions?

He wants us to bring our emotions to him.

I learned this by studying the Psalms and Jesus.

Did you know that nearly one-third of the Psalms fall into the categories of lament and imprecation (calling down God's justice on our enemies)?[9] We tend to focus on the peaceful or comforting psalms, but when we come across a psalmist writing things like, "Happy is the one who takes your babies and smashes them against the rocks" (137:9), we turn the page and say, "Easy there, guy." But the psalmists' hearts reflected God's heart in how they directed their anguish at heaven. Jesus did the same thing on the cross using one of David's laments: "My God, my God, why have you abandoned me?" (Psalm 22:1; Matthew 27:46).

The Father is the safest and most productive place for us to take our suffering.

Too often, we don't go to him first—or at all. Instead, we flit from friend to friend trying to get them to empathize with us. "This is how I feel about my situation!" But no matter who we turn to, no one quite gets it. Our spouse doesn't. Our closest friends don't. Our pastors don't. Proverbs 14:10 alludes to the loneliness we experience in suffering: "Each heart knows its own bitterness, and no one else can fully share its joy." No one else truly understands us. Period.

Some of us know this. We have experienced people's failure and instead of taking our pain to them, we swallow it. But gulping down pain doesn't remove it. Rather, it forces us to reach for emotional antacids, such as overeating, undereating, exercise, drinking, sex, or overworking.

There is a better way. If God allows us to experience pain and negative emotions, it must mean he also created a space where we can take that pain and negative emotion. He is that place. There is no empathizer like Emmanuel, God with us, the inventor of empathy.

When we take our pain to him, we are given the opportunity to experience the character of the God of the Bible. If I need comfort? I can pour out my lack to God in prayer, sit, wait, and envision the comforting God of the Bible showering me with the kind of comfort described in 2 Corinthians 1:3-5.

All praise to God, the Father of our Lord Jesus Christ. God is our merciful Father and the source of all comfort. He comforts us in all our troubles so that we can comfort others. When they are troubled, we will be able to give them the same comfort God has given us. For the more we suffer for Christ, the more God will shower us with his comfort through Christ.

Am I wrestling with toxic shame? I point out areas in my heart to God where I feel less-than and envision the physician who wants me to come to him needy. Jesus came into this world to rescue "not those who think they are righteous, but those who know they are sinners" (Mark 2:17).

When I need his presence to transform any area of suffering, I picture that shackled place and invite God—the one who comes to "comfort the brokenhearted and to proclaim that captives will be released and prisoners will be freed. . . . To all who mourn in Israel, he will give a crown of beauty for ashes, a joyous blessing instead of mourning, festive praise instead of despair" (Isaiah 61:1, 3).

Jesus understands pain. He lamented too. In the Garden of Gethsemane, hours before his death, Jesus essentially said, "God, I don't want to go the cross" (Luke 22:42). Does this read kind of weird to anyone else? Jesus seemed to comfortably step into an "improper" place. Are we allowed to tell God we don't want to do something? Aren't we supposed to say, "Sir, yes, sir," sans emotion? Shouldn't Jesus especially respond that way? I mean, that was his job! "Jesus died on the cross." Christian parents teach it to their children from a young age.

What Jesus did was model for us the right response to suffering: Don't stuff your pain; don't offload it onto your friends to carry for you; offer it to God and invite others to share the burden.

There, he told them, "Pray that you will not give in to temptation."

He walked away, about a stone's throw, and knelt down and prayed, "Father, if you are willing, please take this cup of suffering away from me. Yet I want your will to be done, not mine." Then an angel from heaven appeared and strengthened him. He prayed more fervently, and he was in such agony of spirit that his sweat fell to the ground like great drops of blood.

At last he stood up again and returned to the disciples, only to find them asleep, exhausted from grief. "Why are you sleeping?" he asked them. "Get up and pray, so that you will not give in to temptation." (Luke 22:40-46)

Jesus wanted to lament in community. Laurie and I have engaged in lament many times with other people. We have had the privilege of taking raw, vulnerable hearts to the caretaker of hearts, but we are with them. Lament is best done with others.

Old Testament scholar Bill Bellinger said that the lament psalms are "the backbone of the psalter." And the psalter—a bound collection containing the book of Psalms—held real songs intended to be sung in community. "These most personal of biblical prayers clearly are public prayers," he said. "I often think we mistakenly equate the personal with the private. These personally and communally powerful prayers are part of the community's vibrant worship."[10]

We are meant to lament together.

When we do this, we see two fruits produced. First, we feel *noticed* in those places of deepest pain and shame. Sitting next to Laurie or other friends while pouring my heart out to God helps me to feel less alone in whatever I'm wrestling through. Friends will never get it like God can, but their seeing me helps me to feel God's seeing of me. They reflect Christ.

Second, we are trained to see through people instead of looking to people to meet our needs. Because we are all literally facing God and not each other in prayer, lamenting in community keeps my heart from looking to friends to fix my life. It is harder to make an idol of people while I'm talking to God.

Does this mean we never share our pain without praying?

No. That's weird. We can be normal. But practicing taking our pain in community to the Father trains us to more quickly see through image bearers to God when we are simply talking through life's struggles.

It also helps those who are receiving the words of the person in pain. When we regularly take our pain to God as a group of friends, we are more likely to depend on God to give them encouraging words from him in normal, not-directly-praying conversation.

Before I repented and dove into this intangible world of visual prayer and lament, all I wanted from my relationships was not-prayerful, normal conversation and to be left alone. I thought that somehow staying both isolated and surface level would fix the mess inside. But how can we fix an internal, soul-deep problem with skin-deep solutions?

Jesus wants a relationship with us. He wants to transform us from the inside out. Through visual and lamenting prayer, we can experience this transformation.

It may pull us out of our comfort zones, but through it we can discover that knowing God is worth the discomfort.

NINE

NOT ALONE

In each of my friends there is something that only some other friend can fully bring out. By myself I am not large enough to call the whole man into activity; I want other lights than my own to show all his facets. . . . Hence, true Friendship is the least jealous of loves. Two friends delight to be joined by a third, and three by a fourth.

C. S. LEWIS

LAURIE

We were seeing a lot of growth. God was planting new seeds that were producing fruit.

But this did not happen alone. Behind the scenes we had therapists, mentors, and friends. Our sinful natures wanted to isolate our marriage from the rest of the world, but we knew we couldn't survive isolated. We needed to be a part of the body. And the body was a gift to us. Both single and married friends played integral roles in our healing journey, and we would be remiss to miss their role in this story.

Some new friends were pivotal.

Before the silent retreat and my recommitment to Matt, before taking a Holy Spirit crowbar to the Memory rock, some new friends, Sarah and Ryan, invited us out to dinner. We decided to go—it's a rare gift when both parties in a couple enjoy the company of both people in another couple, but we enjoy them both.

Matt got along well with Ryan, a gangly redhead with a heart of worship and eyes that shed tears quickly for those he loved. They had been in an intensive soul care group with Chris, the husband of my former mentor, Carolyn. Men do not stereotypically dive into the messy areas of the soul together, but Matt, Ryan, and the other men were desperate for something new. Matt's reasoning was that we had recently moved back from California to Michigan and he was only months clean of his pornography addiction. The group challenged Matt's usual cerebral-only way of engaging God, and he enjoyed camaraderie with other guys who were also hesitant but hungry.

I liked Sarah. As a fellow tall, blonde girl, I felt immediate kinship. It was not sexual attraction (I never pursue close friendships with women to whom I'm sexually attracted), but a "kindred spirit" attraction, like Anne describes in the classic *Anne of Green Gables*. "Kindred spirits are not so scarce as I used to think. It's splendid to find out there are so many of them in the world."[1] I felt this connection to Sarah because of her ability to engage me in the strange, deep places of my heart, and because of her natural bent toward dorky fun and silliness. It brought out my own silly side.

Matt and I had slowly begun casting fishing lines of trust to Sarah and Ryan by alluding to some of the depth of our own pain—not all of it but some. Beyond the two of us, no one really knew the reality. It is often terrifying to share your brokenness with others—and our version seemed extra fear-inducing. *Would whomever we told advise we get divorced because I'm not default-attracted to Matt and his gender? Or would they just tell me to have sex with Matt because I'm a bad Christian wife if I don't?* Over time, we saw enough of Sarah and Ryan's theology to know they wouldn't guide us toward divorce and enough of their empathy to know they wouldn't encourage me to "just do it." But we didn't *know* know.

Perhaps tonight we will share. I knew we needed to let someone in. We were barely hanging on.

As we drove to a restaurant to meet Ryan and Sarah, I stared out the window at the darkness and swirling snow. We drove either silently or exchanging logistical information about the kids, work, or schedules. Our hearts were hidden—mine especially. If Matt tried to reach out with a probing question, I stayed quiet. *Maybe if I say nothing his question will go away.* When it did, a part of me felt sad. *Why am I so mean? Why can't I just love him? He's so kind. So many women would go gaga for this incredible man.*

A familiar, quiet voice popped into my head. *Because you aren't attracted to him. You should leave him.* It was the same voice that had helped me to hoard all of my *what-if* candies and files of reasons to leave. Those records were building. The resentment was growing. The motivations to exit piling up.

"Are you excited to hang out with them tonight?" Matt asked, a slightly intrusive question but one that unlocked my jaw. *Try, Laurie.*

"Yeah, I am. I like Sarah." The more words I strung together, the easier it was to talk. *Maybe I do like him.* I looked over at his profile lightened by the streetlamps. *Just like him. Lean in.* My insides curled. *But I don't want to be close to him physically.*

"I am too. I like Ryan," he said. I became quiet again, looking out at the snow globe world. *Ask him a question.* I snapped the lid closed on my heart and locked my jaw. *No. It isn't worth it. It leads to closeness, which leads to physical closeness, and I don't want it. I just want him to be my friend—maybe.*

We arrived at the restaurant around the same time as our friends. We exchanged hugs and before I knew it, both our meals had arrived along with the opportunity to risk relational vulnerability. We had asked about their marriage and the turnaround question faced us.

"How are you guys doing?" they asked.

I stared at my dinner, moisture welling in my eyes. I gritted my teeth, retreating to a place of numbness. It was safer there. Easier. Don't feel. "Not good," I said, detached.

Matt nodded his head in agreement, feeling more than I was. "It's been . . . really hard."

My lips tightened into a straight line. Accusing words tumbled into my mind. It's funny that the same voice that enticed me to leave yelled at me for not wanting to stay. *It's your fault. You are doing this to him. Why can't you pull it together and be connected to him?* Satan doesn't care how he destroys us and the metaphor of marriage. All that matters to him is that he does it.

"We haven't had sex in months," I said. I hated talking about it, but the words needed to break out. As they did, I seemed to watch them crash to the table with a loud bang. The look on Sarah and Ryan's faces told me they had heard them. They looked surprised but . . . aching. *Months? It's been months?*

"Oh, guys," they said, grimacing with empathy. My head dropped again to look at my meal. The accusing voice came back. *Matt wants to have sex. It certainly isn't his fault. It's yours. You are the reason you can't be close physically. You are destroying your marriage.*

I wish I had understood then that the number of times we have sex is just a number. You cannot quantify oneness. The fact that both the world and the church say that sex is the indicator of closeness is a fallacy. Sex can be awash in oneness, but it is not the barometer of it. We had had more sex when Matt was addicted to pornography, but our hearts had been farther away. We had had more sex when I was detaching my brain from by body, but that didn't make us a joyful Ephesians 5 marriage metaphor. We had bodily closeness but not oneness.

It is just like when we do "church stuff"—going several times a week to Bible studies, Sunday mornings, leading groups—but our hearts are not connected to the Father. You cannot quantify oneness with God, and you cannot quantify oneness with your spouse.

But I didn't know that. I saw not having sex as a failure of a marriage. Focusing on that "failure" on my part actually stalled our healing. I felt so much toxic shame for failing at sex that it blinded me from seeing the truth that we were distant in many ways—hearts shut, communication limited, only sometimes on-mission to make disciples together. All of the Gardens of Relating were suffering, but I focused primarily on the physical.

"What percent of hope do you give your marriage right now?" Sarah asked tenderly, her eyes wet with tears.

So much shame poured from me as I opened my mouth to respond. "About 0.6 percent," I said. I gave us less than a percent of hope that we would make it—less than a percent of hope that we would ever thrive.

"Point six?" Sarah asked, surprised again. She let all the air out of her lungs. "Okay. Well. We will stare at the point six until it grows."

"How about you, Matt?" Ryan asked, his face contorted in empathy.

Matt sighed. I looked at him out of the corner of my eye. *Did he have hope for us at all? Please, don't give up. If you give up, I'm toast. I'm barely clinging to that point six.*

"About 5 percent," he said.

I wished it was more. I wished he didn't feel so hurt and that he could be our savior. But he was a person, like me. Not the Savior. And so, combined, we had 5.6 percent of hope for our marriage.

Sarah and Ryan didn't know how to respond.

Their lack of knowing was exactly right.

"Well," Sarah said, smiling through the tears. "We are with you no matter what. We are committed to praying for and with you. We are Team Krieg all the way."

Their lack of answers and commitment to sticking with us was what we needed—it helped remove some of the layers of toxic shame. When we are seen and loved in our mess, the power of this type of shame can be removed from our messy situation.

When self-hating shame is removed, we can get to work on the real issues.

When accusing shame is removed, we can allow people to bear burdens with us like Paul talks about in Galatians 6: "Carry each other's burdens, and in this way you will fulfill the law of Christ. . . . Each one should carry their own load" (vv. 2, 5 NIV).

Where do we carry each other's burdens? Did we need our friends to pick up our pain and put it on their own backs? No. We carry them to Jesus, the one who tells us to come to him when we are weary and burdened, the one who invites us to cast our cares on him (Matthew 11:28; 1 Peter 5:7).

Our friends didn't need to fix our version of an impossible marriage. We simply invited them to be with us in it.

That's important to note: *We invited them.* We did not demand— we invited.

And they said yes.

But here is something else I want to stress: We need to care about each other's marriages because they are a picture of the gospel. Marriages are billboards—at the grocery store, in our neighborhoods, and in our homes—that say, "This is how Jesus loves you." Whether or not we are saying it with our mouths, we are saying it with our love—or lack thereof.

It is a great mystery.

We need to care about each other's billboards. We need not mess with each other's billboards. There is no such thing as innocent flirting. Rolling our eyes about our friend's spouse is not nothing. These "little things" degrade the metaphor. We need to care about marriage as the picture of the gospel that it is.

Sarah and Ryan, other precious couples, and some of our dear single friends did that for us. They understood the seriousness. They got that it was impossible—even our version of impossible.

Because of the public nature of our ministry, most people understand that our marriage is different. *Laurie isn't straight,* they think, *but somehow it works? I don't know.* Our friends knew our public marriage, but they also knew the not-public reality. Matt and I are never false on stages, but the world doesn't always need to know today's suffering. They can know the truth but not the deepest layer of truth. That space of trust needs to be earned.

Sarah and Ryan earned it. We opened the door of our relationship to them, slowly and with care, as they secured our trust with a measure of agony. "Here's the grim reality," we said. It's terrifying to do that in any marriage but perhaps especially in our type of marriage. *What will they say? Encourage divorce because I'm not living my truth? Encourage divorce because Matt deserves someone straight? Offer quick fixes? Minimize the pain? Emphasize the impossibility? Pray the gay away?*

It feels impossible to find friends, pastors, therapists, or *anyone* who is theologically solid, will relate without negating your pain, remains committed to your version of impossible marriage, and will take your burdens with you to Jesus. But each of these caring pieces was critical for us.

Let's go through each one: theologically solid. Many in our generation have not studied God's design for marriage. They simply *instinctively feel* same-sex marriage is either wrong or right. When our marriage was on the rocks, Matt and I needed more than instinct. We needed friends with a theological backbone to gently oppose us when one of us said, "This is what I want." Did they have enough theological grounding to stand up to my fiery self or Matt's grieving self with the truth? I needed that. The spirit in us needed and truly wanted that.

Granted, our friends never had to be so bold as to say, "Laurie, Matt, this is what is true about marriage," but because they had studied, I knew they wouldn't waver even if we did.

The next criterion: they will relate but not negate your pain. "Laurie, I don't know all of the wrestling you are going through," Sarah might have said, "but I can understand a tiny bit about how you feel so frustrated at Matt when it comes to this or that . . ." She related but didn't negate it. This helped me to feel like another, regular old impossible marriage with specific marriage pain.

The third helpful piece in people who care for our marriage is that they are committed to our version of an impossible marriage. "We don't know how God is going to do this," many of our friends said, "but we are with you. We are all in." That was it. That "I'm here no matter what" backbone paired with the theology of God's design for marriage was gigantic. It helped us to feel like we did not have to hold our marriage together on our own. We could put all of our cards on the table, wrestling with every piece of it while knowing God was for us, as people—the body of Christ—"carried" our metaphor with us. We didn't have to wrestle with it while carrying it on our own.

The last critical piece in people who care for our version of an impossible marriage is that they take our burdens to Jesus. To take something to Jesus you have to touch it—like Jesus. He was not afraid of getting his hands dirty or associating with people who were scorned by the religious (Luke 7:34; 15:2). He touched people's pain, mess, and literal leprosy (Matthew 8:3). Our friends did that too. They held our suffering. They were not scared of us. They were not afraid of themselves around us. They did not think, "Oh, if I get too close to this pain, then I'll change my mind theologically." Or, "I don't want to make Laurie stumble by hugging her."[2] Or, "This is just too hard." They knew it was too hard, too big, impossible, but they believed, even when we didn't, that our impossible wasn't too impossible for Jesus. They were with us in the impossible journey.

There are some who have abandoned us in our journey. Not everyone responds like Sarah and Ryan. I have shared my story and had people respond by saying they don't want me around their kids anymore, as if my attractions make me a pedophile. Some have said our journey is "too much" and referred me to counseling. Maybe I did need counseling, but I also needed friends.

Others have mysteriously stopped calling or reaching out. When pressed they said, "It's your story. I just . . . I don't know how to be friends with you." The speaker is often a female and they see me as a threat. Because I am attracted to females, I must be attracted to them. As a heterosexual person, are they attracted to every one of the opposite sex?

I have had people try to rescue me from my marriage. They try to get me alone, away from Matt to say, "You just need to find a good wife. Be you." They think they are setting me free, but how can they liberate me outside of God's path of flourishing?

Those we let into our inner circle didn't do any of that. They were *with us*.

One with us—with me—time I'll never forget.

Months had passed since praying through the Memory, and I was grieving because I still could not connect physically with Matt. I thought once the rock of the Memory was gone, I would be healed. It would be a slow, upward progression toward physical oneness. But it wasn't.

We were still stuck.

I left the house one morning to run with Sarah without saying goodbye to Matt. My heart was more connected to his than . . . well, it likely had ever been. He was porn-free. I was nearly detachment free. But the report card was still present: Having sex means you're passing your marriage. Not having sex means failing.

I let myself cry the whole drive out but wiped my face before jumping out of the car to greet Sarah. How quickly we forget that safe people will even love us in our messes.

We hit the literal pavement running, but after about a mile of chitchatting, I couldn't hold it together anymore. We entered a dark, brooding green canopy of forest, and it felt like a needed hug—a needed hug that drew out tears.

I obliged, stopping, gripping my knees, and let the sobs out.

"I'm still frozen! Why? I love him so much, but I can't move forward physically with him!"

Sarah put a gentle hand on my back. She knew I was not a touchy person but also recognized my need for touch in that moment. It was comforting, not scary. Her hand said, "I see you. I am with you. I represent the one who is safe." She saw me in this deep place of mess and removed shame so that we could get to the real issues beneath the shame.

After minutes of weeping, we began to run again—mosquitos don't take breaks for emotional breakdowns.

"What do you want, Laurie?" she asked. "Do you want to be able to have sex with him?"

What do I want? That question again. Now, a year after the snowstorm silent retreat. How different my heart had become. "I want to look like Jesus," I said. "I want to love Matt like Jesus loves him. I want to show Matt that Jesus loves him holistically— that he wants to be one with him."

It sounded altruistic, but I really meant it. But my motives were not 100 percent pure. There was another reason for my desire to connect with him physically: the report card. The performance-based idol I bowed down to, often unknowingly, every day. *Once we have sex, I get an A+ on marriage. Once we have sex, I am okay.*

"Have you asked God what he wants for you in this season?" Sarah asked.

What kind of question was that? Of course, God wants us to have sex. Doesn't Paul tell us to "not deprive each other of sexual relations" (1 Corinthians 7:5)?

Granted, I wasn't intentionally depriving Matt. I was unable to connect with him as much as I tried. The Memory rock was gone, but I was still blocked.

Didn't God just want me to remove that blockage? Isn't he crazy about physical connection? I mean, the world and the church seem to be. So, isn't God?

What do you want, God?

After our run, I showered and found a corner in a coffee shop to journal and pray through the question with the Father.

God, what do you want? I am willing to do anything for you. I do not believe it is your will that I feel violated by forcing myself to be close to Matt. You don't want me to shut down parts of me to be close to you or Matt. You don't want me to detach again. But I don't know how to move forward. What do you want? Isn't sex with Matt your greatest desire for me?

Then I heard it: "Oh, dear Laurie. My greatest desire for you is to be one with me. But you can't be one with me and bow to your performance-centered identity."

Wait a minute. Performance-centered identity? What did he mean?

Healing the trauma wasn't God's primary goal for my life. Getting me to surrender my sexuality was not God's primary goal for my life. Having sex with Matt was not God's primary goal for my life. God's primary goal for me and for the church is to be one with us—and that that oneness tells the world of his love.

But we can only be one if there is nothing between us. God is holy, so he can't hang out with sin—even sin disguised as holiness, such as "Once I can have sex with Matt, *then I will be okay.*"

Any statement that begins with, "Once I have" or "If only" is an idol statement. And idols—even altruistic idols—keep us from oneness with God.

"Precious Laurie," God seemed to whisper to my heart. "You are not okay once you can have sex with Matt. You are not okay once your trauma is healed. You are not okay if you aren't wrestling with whatever version of sexual brokenness. Your okayness comes when I declare you mine—and I say you are mine. I love you right now—even if you never have sex again. I love you no matter what. You can't earn this grace. You can't earn this love. It is a free, undeserved gift."

I was stunned. As much as we say, "I'm saved by grace," it's much harder to live like it. We work for it. We baptize our performance idols in Christianese.

God continued: "Will you take this grace gift right now? Will you let me love you right now? As you are? In your 'failing in the sex report card' state?"

I looked out of the window of my corner of the coffee shop. *I will try, God. I will try. I choose to open my heart up to you. Take our marriage where you want it—whether or not we have sex again. You are enough for me. Let me believe it not only this minute but the next and next and next.*

I was starting to get it. God did not cause trauma; God did not create me broken; God did not want marriage pain—but he was using it all.

He wasn't even using it so that I'd become an expert at navigating suffering (a performance-based identity). He was using it to show me his grace is enough.

This was rich. This was new. But I do not believe I would have been able to hear or receive it had we not allowed friends in who could see us in our mess, love us in our mess, and, therefore, remove the power of shame so that we could get to the real issues below the surface.

• • •

MATT

We didn't get through the most grueling parts of our marriage journey on our own. Friends were with us. Before we even invited them in, however, I invited my dad.

I needed to hear his voice—his affirmation. I don't know how to explain it, other than it felt coded into my DNA. "I need my dad."

As much as he is an amazing man of God, I was scared to call him. What would he say? Would he judge me? Judge her? Tell me platitudes? He knew the nuances of our relationship—her attractions, my former addiction—but it's still always risky to be the one in need. Not the one educating about "the issues" but the one in need when these issues hit home.

In her book *The Gifts of Imperfection*, Brené Brown lists responses to pain that are unhelpful. I definitely feared these before talking with my dad or anyone about our marriage:

1. The friend who hears and responds with gasps. They are shocked and appalled and shame your shame with big eyes and an open mouth.

2. The friend who does not respond with empathy ("I get it, I feel with you, and I've been there") but with sympathy ("I feel so sorry for you").

3. The friend who can't handle that you are not the mantle of perfection she thought you were. You've disappointed her.

4. The friend who can't handle vulnerability, so they scold you. "How could you let that happen?"

5. The friend who wants to make it better, so they cover it up. "You're exaggerating; it wasn't that bad."

6. The friend who one-ups you. "That's nothing. Listen to what happened to me!"[3]

I didn't need any of those reactions. Thankfully, I didn't get any of them from my dad.

Our kids were napping, and Laurie was washing the dishes. You could cut the hostile waves she was sending my direction with a knife. This was before the marriage intensive, before praying through the Memory, before inviting friends on the journey, and before much of the ice in our home melted.

My hope meter was at 0.1 percent that day. I felt like she hated me. There was no warmth. There was no kindness. Sex had been off the table for months, and I was in a season of simply seeking friendship. No pursuit of anything physical, just kindness—but even that seemed impossible.

I thought about whom I could talk to about this relational fissure. Laurie had forbidden me from opening up totally to our new friends, Sarah and Ryan, since she didn't know if we could trust them yet. She was terrified that people would judge and shame us, so she put a lockbox on our ability to communicate with others.

I wanted to honor her desire but felt I would die under the weight of our broken marriage. After an abrasive conversation with Laurie, she permitted me to talk to my dad. "He gets it, Laurie," I said with gentleness. I understood her fear of being judged and shamed, but I also knew—well, hoped—that other marriages could relate to us more than we realized. "He's been through a lot, and I could use an understanding friend right now."

Her eyes narrowed. She got the inference. *Laurie, you are not my friend right now.* I knew—well, hoped—she still loved me, but her pain was isolating us from others.

I walked out onto the deck and down to the swing set in our backyard. I sat down beside the slide, called my dad, and buried my head in my arms.

"Hey, Dad," I said, my voice cracking.

"Hey, son!" he responded joyfully. Something about hearing the voice of the man who has championed me from before the day I was born pulled at my heartstrings. I let the tears fall.

"Dad . . ." I couldn't say the rest of the sentence.

"What, son?" he said, his concern growing.

"I think we are done. I don't know how we are going to make it."

"You and Laurie?"

"Yeah. I don't know if we will ever have joy in our home again. I think she's going to leave. She seems to hate me."

I heard him cough, tying to dislodge a sob catching in his throat. He so loved Laurie and me.

"How did you do it, Dad? How *do* you do it?" My parent's marriage has had some prolonged seasons of suffering. My dad would pursue, my mom would detach. That was their pattern for years. But my dad never gave up. He never stopped saying how much he adored and loved her. He was faithful, even when she was often very cold.

I needed to learn from his openhearted resilience. "How do you do it?" I asked again, desperate.

He paused. "Matt, first of all, I'm sorry that you're going through this. And secondly, how do I do it? Well, I had to give up looking to your mom to make me happy a long time ago." He cleared his throat again, finding a path through his empathetic tears. "I keep my heart open to your mom but have my focus on Jesus. God is my sustaining relationship—not Patty. He gives me my joy—not my marriage."

It sounded like he was speaking a foreign language.

He wasn't done. "I don't turn away from your mom, but I don't face her to give me life and love. I face God, and then I turn to her to pour out his love onto her."

I wiped my face with the back of my hand and then picked at the grass. "It isn't easy," he continued, sighing. I was certain it was impossible. "It is a challenge, but I sure have grown close to God because of it, and I have more love for your mom now than I have ever had. Jesus gives it to me."

How? How could it be? This receiving-nothing-but-still-pouring-out love sounded impossible without supernatural intervention. How can we love those who give us nothing—like in real life?

It sounded like death.

An image came to mind. Of course, it did. The ultimate death. The ultimate love sacrifice: Jesus on the cross—literally dying for us. We gave him nothing, and he offered us everything. He wanted oneness with us so much that he died.

How could he do that? We deserved death, but he died. How could he love us that deeply?

Grace—amazing grace.

God? I prayed after hanging up with my dad. *Could you please give me some of that love? Some of that grace? I can't do this without you. I can't love Laurie without you. Please, help me.*

He did.

I began praying more than I ever had. I put more energy into fasting from my desire for sex and asking God to help me remove all of the barriers between him and those places of need in my heart.

And he didn't leave me hanging. Some days left me feeling like a desert—empty, dry, and borderline hated while seeking to remove weeds so that God's love could pour into Laurie. She hardly noticed. But some days the Holy Spirit made it easier. He cut through all of the barriers and poured into my own empty soul so that it could receive fullness. On those easy cultivating days, I felt deeply noticed, desired, and loved by God.

Sometimes, he used friendships to emphasize this reality.

After opening up about our marriage over dinner with Sarah and Ryan, Laurie and I started a small group with them and another couple, Kerri and Caleb. All of us wanted more than a usual Christian gathering where the people show up, share potlucks, maybe read a book, but never truly become each other's spiritual family. We all were starving for life-on-life, soul-searching, Jesus-seeking friendships.

I think most people are searching for this. It just takes enormous effort to create and find. Praise God, Laurie was hungry enough for Jesus and real friendship to risk inviting these other couples to the deep, small group table.

They, along with Jason and Julie, a third couple who joined a year later, became critical to our healing journey. They were the ones we could go to when life came crashing down, and they could come to us when their lives hit the fan. Our model was simple: each couple takes a turn leading by asking God how to dive in. Sometimes, we opened up as couples to share how we were doing while the others prayed and listened for verses, words, or pictures to speak over us. Some weeks, we read a passage of Scripture and offered what stood out. Sometimes, we took marriage evaluations and reflected on areas of needed growth. There were weeks we just worshiped. Other times, we broke up into groups of men and women to share and pray over our lives and marriages.

During weeks when we split into separate groups, I experienced the love of Jesus with the guys. So often in our relationships, especially with our spouse, we can be goal-oriented: set budgets, make life goals, plan a vacation, save for retirement, pursue growth, raise the kids, go to church, do the schedule. These aren't inherently bad things—but they are a lot of work.

I didn't need more work. I needed brothers. Friends. Because I so often felt disliked in my house, I appreciated when the guys and I just talked about nothing. We could spend two hours in conversation and come away joking about how much we love chicken wings and building fires. Checking in on our souls is equally as important as the silliness.

Both joking and weeping with friends told my aching heart, "We love you, Matt. We enjoy you—as you. You can be real here." They let me rest. I didn't feel I had to hold my breath and watch my every move like I did at home. They liked me and represented the One who likes me.

But they didn't save me. They didn't become the ones I looked to for my security. My identity was (as best as I could) based on what Jesus did for me on the cross. If I focused my eyes on my friends rather than Jesus, God, in his mercy, would let them fail me so that I would remember they are not the ones upon whom I am to base my worth.

But their support was helpful. In their presence, I was reminded of my worth. The enemy wanted to resurrect the lie that he spoke over me before I was born. *See? Even the woman who covenanted for life with you sees you for who you are: totally worthless.* But friendships with my brothers at this small group and those outside of it helped me to see the lies for what they were.

I am not worthless. I am loved—as me. I don't have to earn it. No matter what Laurie thought of me, my brothers, my friends, and my dad represented the older brother, the best friend, and the Father who loves me—just as I am (John 15:15; Romans 8:15-16, 29).

God was using this suffering to do something good in me. Suffering shredded the lie that said, "You are worthless." Suffering was teaching me to truly love people, not for what they could give me but because of God's love for them through me.

Suffering was producing fruit in me.

Could it do the same in our marriage?

TEN

A GOSPEL PICTURE

The reason that marriage is so painful and yet wonderful is because it is a reflection of the gospel, which is painful and wonderful at once. The gospel is this: We are more sinful and flawed in ourselves than we ever dared believe, yet at the very same time we are more loved and accepted in Jesus Christ than we ever dared hope.

TIM KELLER

LAURIE

When our second daughter, Juliette, was born, I set my heart against having another child. Blearily walking down our hallway in the middle of the night for what felt like the thousandth time to silence her screams, I yelled at Matt over my shoulder, "You can't make me have another kid!"

"I can't make you do anything!" he said. I mean . . . he wasn't wrong.

This was before the Memory resurfaced. This was before our marriage almost ended.

Now, two years later, I heard a whisper in my heart. *Another baby. You are supposed to have another baby.*

Well, joke's on you, God, because we can't have sex unless you are into traumatizing people.

But would it be a trauma? Would being physically close with Matt at this point—years into our confrontation with deep pain and many months into an upward growth of healing—be traumatic?

Since the visual prayer of the Memory, we started over physically. Like . . . completely. Sure, we had had two kids, but I wanted to walk our physical relationship backward to ensure my mind, body, and spirit were present every time I engaged with Matt in any way.

But before we restarted, I did something gentle and important for my soul: I said sorry to it. I apologized for every time I had pushed myself faster and further than I was ready dating all the way back to junior high when the cool boy liked me and inched his hand toward mine during the theater release of *Star Wars: Episode 1.* I ended up just grabbing his hand and holding it to put myself in control. *I'm sorry, Laurie,* I wrote to myself. *I'm sorry for pushing you.* I wrote down every mild and major sexual encounter I had that the Lord brought to mind where I pushed myself and apologized to Jesus and to myself. This and all of the other work we had done prepared us to move forward holistically.

Matt and I started with holding hands and did not progress any further for weeks. Considering that for several years I had despised Matt's physical presence, hardly touching him at all in even friendly ways, handholding was pretty forward. But once I became comfortable with that step, I moved us onto the next one: hugs. I became okay with hugging briefly in front of the kids and embracing slightly longer on our own. Kissing came weeks later. Again, brief pecks in front of the kids and slightly longer in private.

But during these months of glacial progression, Matt and I were intent on communicating about it. It felt awkward. "What does this hug mean?" I asked. But I wanted and needed the questions. Matt did not want a body-only wife, and I did not want to be a body-only wife. We wanted oneness—every garden full of life, the Holy Spirit pouring into every connection.

Additionally, if I shut my brain down and engaged physically, we would end up right back where we began our healing journey.

So, we talked awkwardly. "Laurie, are you present? How are you feeling?" Matt asked frequently. It often took me a minute to evaluate my integration. *How am I? Am I here?* I often silently spoke truth to myself because I truly desired to be one with him, even if our physical oneness was only hugging. *Matt's desire for me physically is good. He is showing me God's desire to be totally one with me, and I show the same to him.* "I'm okay," I said honestly. "I'm really doing well."

There was no rushing. No pushing. Just gentleness. We engaged in a slow, integrated, physical progression. It felt like we were dating, but I didn't judge myself for going backward. I encouraged myself because I was *choosing now.* I was present now.

But even though I was progressing slowly, the "have another baby" whisper baffled me. We had tried to move forward toward total physical connection since the Memory had resurfaced, and again since the freeing visual prayer, but it had left me paralyzed—hence the weeping on my run with Sarah. But as I reflected on those attempts, I saw I had been pushing myself beyond slow progression. Doing so risked causing us to have to start again from square one.

However, more months had passed since my breakdown on the run with Sarah, and I had been obeying my own rule to walk slowly enough to stay integrated. *Engage all of the gardens. What Core Need is blocked? How is your need to be protected doing?*

I was also adding in the newfound depth of understanding God's grace for me. *No matter what, sex or no sex, I am loved. I am not failing at marriage. I am not a failure. I am equally loved. You cannot quantify oneness. Pursue oneness with Matt. Show Matt how much Jesus loves him and allow Matt to show you how much Jesus loves you—in ways you feel comfortable.*

As I received God's grace, and as we slowly moved forward, I found our spiritual and relational oneness leading me toward a real desire to be with him completely. Detached Laurie didn't desire this. Holistic, integrated Laurie did.

This was new. And weird.

On another run, I shared my secret thoughts with Sarah. "I think God wants us to have another baby."

She stopped, turned, and looked me in the eyes with tears brimming.

"I haven't wanted to say anything because you need zero pressure on you, but I felt like God told me to pray that over you yesterday," she said. "It was so strange, Laurie." Sarah went on to explain that the day before she had started thinking about our upcoming run. "The Lord suddenly dropped something in my heart. 'Pray for another baby for Matt and Laurie.' I was shocked. I knew the challenges you faced, but I sensed that God wanted to use the prayer of a baby to take the focus off of the physical-only part of sex and onto the bigger, fruitful picture."

Somehow, I wasn't surprised. *Of course, you would tell my friends, God.* He loves us too much to leave us alone. "I started praying into it but told God I wouldn't breathe a word of it to you. But then you said it! You said it first!"

She hugged me and while she did, I looked over her shoulder toward the familiar path we had just run. We had counted so many miles on that trail, talking, crying, begging Jesus for a miracle in my impossible marriage.

It was a miracle that Matt and I were still married.

It would be a miracle if God chose to bring about a baby from this marriage.

A few days later, I took my journal to a coffee shop to hash it out with God.

God? I want to give you everything. I am learning to trust you. But why should I pursue this?

He was quick to respond.

"Could it be possible, dear one, that I want to teach you *more* about the gospel through sex with Matt?"

I stopped and stared out of the window from the barstool where I sat. Then I wrote some more:

That terrifies me. Completely.

"Can you trust me? Can you trust me with you?"

Can I? I thought over the last few years. Every time I had surrendered my life to him, it resulted in both pain and growth. Pain
and growth—like labor.

But didn't I choose our marriage? I did. Did I choose wrongly?
No—and yes. We all marry the "wrong" person. But even though
that is true, I know God was in it. I know he called us together.

"Do you think your marriage was an accident?" He seemed to
say. "Do you think I was looking the other way? Do you think you
forced something outside of my will? And even if you somehow
were able to work outside of my will, do you think I can't make
everything work for the good for those who love me and live
according to my good purposes? If you, in good faith and heart,
made choices you believed were right and honoring to me, don't
you think I can make those right and good?"

This, God? You can do this, too? You know the blocks I have.

"Do you know what else was a block? The cross."

Well, he wasn't wrong.

"I turned that block of wood used for torture into a symbol
of life."

I sighed and continued writing down what I sensed him
saying to me.

"Do you think I can use this block in your marriage? Do you
think I can use this symbol that the world rips to shreds as a
symbol of my grace for you? I want to show you more of me in
your sexual relationship to Matt."

*What? I don't know how to believe it, God! I want to . . . I don't
know how it is possible.*

"I can do anything, Laurie. You have nothing to fear. Nothing is
impossible with me."

I paused, listened again, and wrote.

"Watch me, Laurie. Watch me love you."

A few days later, I did.

I was working on my laptop while Matt washed the dishes. He
had come home from a long day of counseling clients, but he still
served our family. Statistics show that 84 percent of women use

sex to get their husbands to do more around the house, and men likely do more around the house to get sex but not in our home.[1] To use sex as currency would not have been glorifying to God. It would have only reinforced my detachment. Matt served us because we are called to love selflessly as Christians.

After he was done, he poured himself a drink and went downstairs to watch TV. I sensed God prompting me to put away my work and join him. Old Laurie would never have listened and gone down to be in Matt's presence. Old Laurie would have kept working or gone to bed. I grabbed a beverage and some dark chocolate and joined him to watch a cooking show.

While we watched, drank, and ate chocolate, we folded laundry. Three loads together. Then we sat somewhat closely. Old Laurie would never have gotten so physically close to him. Old Laurie would have kept to her side of the couch. But I sat within a foot of him. He noticed and smiled. He didn't push me. He just smiled. It felt safe.

My need to be protected was barrier-free. The family, social, and stewardship gardens were getting cultivated as we cared for the family and watched a stupid show, all the while being frugal about it.

When the program was over, we clicked off the TV and headed upstairs to bed. I kept my ears open to God. I sensed him telling me something that felt like it was only a half step ahead of me. "Laurie, dear one. Be with him. This is the time. I want you to have another baby."

I could almost hear the Holy Spirit rain on our mountain—bringing life to all of the gardens.

After getting ready for bed, I laid next to Matt. I let him hold me. Old Laurie would not have done this. Old Laurie would have turned away from him silently, thrown my sleep mask over my eyes, and slipped off to sleep immediately. But I stayed. No movement. Just letting him hold me. Matt had no expectations—I knew this. He had learned these two years to let me lead. Let me be where I can be. Let me choose him. It's so important for formerly traumatized people to make these kinds of choices.

I felt safe.

"Can you pray?" I asked. Hey there, spiritual garden.

We had prayed many times before any small physical inter-action. To hear Matt connect with the Holy Spirit alleviated any fear. Matt was not nearly as triggering and frightening to me as he had been in the past, but God was not triggering at all. He gave me real peace.

Matt prayed, rejecting any darkness in our room and inviting God into this space. As he did, I could hear God more plainly.

"You can learn something about my intense love for you in your sexual relationship with Matt."

I could sense angels over our bed like an arch ascending to eternity. I could tell they were high up and yet right here— cheering us on.

Sex can be awash in oneness.

It still took trust. It was not perfect. I had tears in my eyes the whole time.

I thought many things. *I'm not crying because I'm triggered. I'm crying because I am so grateful.* I thought of all the times when lying in the same bed as Matt filled me with self-hatred, fear, and contempt toward him. Now there was openness and a desire for deeper-than-physical connection—and also physical connection.

But this isn't perfect. The thought slammed into me. *I am not perfect. I didn't shower. I stink. I don't look cute. We aren't away on a vacation somewhere.* In my visions of this moment, I pictured a tropical location. This was a Tuesday at home.

God knew my thoughts. "That's the point, dear one. You don't have to be perfect; you just have to come to me. You don't have to have it all together; you just need to receive my grace. This is the gospel: You are more sinful than you know and more loved than you can imagine. And through your sin and beauty, I still want you. I desire oneness with you."

That is what sex is? Oneness made tangible? Oneness made fleshy? Even though we stink, even though we are sinners, the Word became flesh to be one with us forever. And one day we will be.

How in the world do people treat sex so tritely? How could it be a part of a film? How can people have a one-night stand? Sex includes the husband and wife, but it isn't only about the husband and wife. They get the opportunity to image to and with each other God's covenant gospel love.

After, I wept.

"Are you okay?" Matt asked, slightly panicked. How many times had his slight touch triggered sobbing and weeks of pain between us?

"I'm not crying because I'm sad," I said, shocked at my lack of desire to cower. "I'm crying because I can't believe we are here." I wiped tears from my eyes. "I am so grateful."

He kissed the top of my head. I smiled. "This feels like our honeymoon," I said.

"It does." He smiled too.

I thought this was impossible.

It was—without Jesus.

It was a slow progression. It took study. It took gritty, inner heart work. But I learned something through the process that I thought I already knew. I am a sinner, I am loved, and Jesus died for me so that we can be one forever.

Sex with my husband taught me a deeper layer of the gospel's good news.

• • •

MATT

I thought it was impossible.

It was—without Jesus.

I could not believe she wanted to move forward. I couldn't believe I was able to slow it down.

Through the years of our physical separation, I had to learn sacrificial love. It was the only way I could not just survive my marriage but love Laurie through it. I was beyond tempted to close off my heart and repay evil for evil, but with the advice from my dad and the exhortation of Scripture, I cut open my broken heart to receive God's love and pour it back onto Laurie.

If our husband/wife relationship is to model the Jesus/church relationship, I am supposed to lay down my life for my wife.

This does not mean doing the dishes so that I can get some. It means doing the dishes because I am called to serve her, even when she is acting unkindly.

This does not mean I serve the family all day long and then in the bedroom say, "Yay! It's me time." Loving Laurie like Jesus means serving her, even in the bedroom.

That selfless sex perspective radically changed us. It helped her to move forward, helped me to stop triggering her, and made me more Christlike.

But it took deep heart work to get there. One picture God gave to help me better understand my own heart when it came to sex was the story of the Samaritan woman at the well. In John 4:4, the writer says Jesus "had to go through Samaria." However, historians say that there was no geographical reason Jesus *had* to go through Samaria. Jews often skirted the entire area to avoid interacting with the Samaritans who they viewed as a mixed race of pagan people with whom pious Jews did not interact.[2]

Not Jesus. The phrase "had to go" comes from the Greek word *dei*. It means "must needs" or "it is absolutely necessary." We see this same word used in relationship to Jesus' necessity to suffer and die in Luke 17:25: "But first the Son of Man must suffer terribly and be rejected by this generation." That was a big picture *dei*—Jesus *must* suffer for us—and this was a big picture *dei*: Jesus *had* to go to Samaria.

So why did he have to go? I believe it was because he knew who was worth seeking there. This was a woman who felt such shame and worthlessness that she came to draw water "about noontime" (John 4:6) in the heat of the day, to avoid interacting with the other women who drew water in the cool of the morning. Perhaps she felt she had to avoid others because of her marital status—five husbands in her past and the man she lived with wasn't her husband. She was a pariah in the midst of a group of shunned people. This woman was the worst of the worst.

But Jesus cut through racial, religious, and social barriers to seek her out. "Please give me a drink" he asked her (4:7). Jewish people considered such an act "as if he ate swine's flesh."[3] Jesus didn't care. He humbled himself and asked her for a drink.

The request led to a conversation about religious practices, tangible water, and living water. Eventually, Jesus named the thing for which this woman truly thirsted: the Messiah. The Savior. The God-man in front of her who could actually fill the well of need in her aching, shame-covered heart. Her eyes were opened to the Jesus who could quench her eternal thirst in such a way that the woman "left her water jar beside the well and ran back to the village, telling everyone . . . [and] many Samaritans from the village believed in Jesus" (John 4:28, 39).

But what came before all of that? What came before her awakening to her thirst for Jesus? Jesus' humble, gentle, patient pursuit.

His thirst for her came first.

When I understood this, it hit me like a truck. Marriage is not about an exchange of goods: her body for my heart. Marriage— scratch that—our whole lives are about serving first.

I am to love Laurie no matter what, just like Jesus loves me no matter what. If she rejects me, I trained myself to ask, "How many times do I reject Jesus?" And yet just like he went out of his way for the woman at the well, he went out of his way for me. How many times do I say to Jesus, "Not you, Jesus, but me. My will be done"? Yet his arms outstretched on the cross tells me, "Not you, Matt. But me. I'll take the punishment for you. I'll go first."

His thirst for me came first.

I took these humble images of Jesus at the well and on the cross and put them next to my heart. Every time Laurie pushed me away, every time she froze me out, I reached in empathy to my co-sufferer, Jesus, and I prayed:

Jesus, do you understand what it feels like to be rejected?

"Oh, I do."

And yet you still come to us for water, asking humbly rather than demanding?

"Oh, yes, brother Matt."

And you don't make us pay if we reject you?

"No, I don't."

You still pursue?

"Yes."

Then I can too. Your empathy encourages me. Your empathy helps me to release my death grip on what I think I need for what I truly need—your love and your desire for me.

It was a Tuesday night, and Laurie was working on the computer while I cleaned the kitchen.

I reflected silently on how much our hearts had grown closer. Even this silent, side-by-side work had a certain warmth and calmness to it. "We are better friends and our marriage is more solid without sex than with it," I had recently said to her. It was true. We laughed more and had deeper conversations with sex as a *maybe . . . someday . . . if we are able* option than as the focus of our lives.

I had given Laurie all of the power over any progression of our physical relationship. I wanted her to know she had control. She could trust me. I may have been physically stronger, but I surrendered my strength.

We started over with handholding. Any movement Laurie made toward me was extremely meaningful. I knew what it cost for her to pat my back in affirmation publicly. I understood how monumental it was the first time she could hold my hand while walking down our neighborhood sidewalk. I savored when she kissed me as I left for work instead of giving me a side hug. I treasured it because I knew the work it took for her to get there and that she was present in that moment. Each tiny movement toward me was a gift that said, *I see you, Matt. I like you. You aren't worthless. This is how God feels about you. He sees you. He likes you. He says you have so much worth. He wants to be one with you.*

When I finished wiping off the counters, I grabbed a drink and went downstairs to watch *MasterChef*—one of our favorites. I didn't invite her but not out of spite or fear. Old Matt would have slunk downstairs alone, afraid and closed off because he didn't want to be relationally or physically rejected again. New Matt, however, kept his heart open. You can feel that sort of openheartedness in the air, even if you aren't saying, "You are welcome with me." I hoped she could feel the gentle invitation to just . . . be with me.

I was happily surprised when she came down to join me on the couch. I was even more pleased when she sat closer to me than usual and offered a half smile. Old Matt would have taken this as a signal to reach out to her in some way—notice her, talk with her, or gently scratch her back to subtly set the stage for something later.

Not New Matt. New Matt did not try to alter the mood so that he could feel desired. New Matt saw her risk toward me, treasured the tiny movement, and responded with a grateful smile. No expectation, just a smile.

Love does not coerce. Jesus does not coerce.

He invites. He is present. He is ready and available, but he does not prepare a way for us so that he can steal from us. He does not say, "Now that they are in church, it's me time." Jesus is self-sacrificing.

I am to be self-sacrificing.[4]

When we moved up toward the bedroom and she lay down next to me, I continued to surrender any expectations to God. I was so grateful for the months—years—of learning to do so by fasting from my desire for sex. *God, I am not going to sit here and pine after Laurie,* I often prayed. *I give her to you. I surrender my desire. I want to desire you more than anything else.*

When Laurie asked me to pray, I was grateful. Old Matt would have prayed begrudgingly. *I'm ready to rock and roll here, Laurie! Why are you making me change my brain from my sexual desires to God? Way to kill the mood.* Now, I understood that I was wrong to separate God from sex. All of it belongs to him. True oneness sex can only happen with the Holy Spirit's involvement.

I invited the Spirit into our room, rejected the enemy from that space, and asked for peace.

As we moved forward, I did what I had learned to do in the previous two years and checked in with her. "Laurie, are you sure you are okay with this step? Are you pushing yourself or is God encouraging you to?" I had to fight my flesh so hard, but I knew it was right.

I did not want to repeat the lessons porn had taught me—that sex is only about physical pleasure. The other gardens don't matter. Idolize your needs, don't open them up for God to fill. You only care for the other person because you know the turnaround is about you.

I didn't want to have self-centered sex. I wanted oneness.

So even though my hormones wanted to move forward, I made sure she was present and I prayed.

God, you want to be one with us. You sacrificed yourself to be one with us, and you will be one with us. God, you want to show Laurie your desire to be one with her. Thank you for showing me this and for allowing me to show her this through this expression.

Sex is about physical touch, to be sure, but it is about far more than physical touch. It is about what is going on *inside* us . . . sex becomes a form of physical prayer—a picture of a heavenly intimacy that rivals the *shekinah* glory of old. Our God, who is spirit (John 4:24), can be found behind the very physical panting, sweating, and pleasurable entangling of limbs and body parts. He doesn't turn away. He wants us to run into sex, but to do so with his presence, priorities, and virtues making our pursuit. If we experience sex this way, we will be transformed in the marriage bed every bit as much as we are transformed on our knees in prayer.[5]

It was not perfect, but it was just right, and it was so different from what I had experienced with pornography and with Laurie for the first eight years of our marriage.

So different.

Sex with my wife now taught me a deeper layer of the gospel's good news.

ELEVEN

NEW LIFE

I tell you the truth, you will weep and mourn over what is going to happen to me, but the world will rejoice. You will grieve, but your grief will suddenly turn to wonderful joy. It will be like a woman suffering the pains of labor. When her child is born, her anguish gives way to joy because she has brought a new baby into the world. So you have sorrow now, but I will see you again; then you will rejoice, and no one can rob you of that joy.

JOHN 16:20-22

LAURIE

Not long afterward, I started noticing pregnancy signs. I took a test, and it was positive. I took another, and it was negative. I wondered and prayed . . .

Meanwhile, Matt's mom's health began fading. Patty was sixty-one but had been using an oxygen tank to breathe for almost two years. Days after we visited for what would be her last birthday party, Matt's parents left on a month-long road trip and Alaskan cruise. Patty had been talking about this vacation for the entire decade I had known her.

A few days before they returned, I said to Matt, "I wonder if when she gets back, she will go to see Jesus. She took her dream trip, and then it will be time for her to take her trip into eternity."

She collapsed in their driveway the night they came home and passed away two weeks later.

The weekend she died, I felt cramping and miscarried.

So much death.

I thought oneness produced fruit. I thought fruit was what we were trying to cultivate in our stupid gardens.

I started to back up from Matt. To cower. To fear. *Oh no,* I thought. *I risked, and it didn't produce Disney! It produced death.*

I grieved Patty's death and silently grieved the death of the baby. Hardly anyone knew.

Everything looked grey. *Why all of this work? Why all of this effort if it only left me sad? Empty. No fruit.*

I took to my journal.

I want to push everyone away. I want to hide in a ball. I don't want to pursue anyone. I don't want to give. I want to hide. I hear you saying, "Laurie, when you cut off your heart from the world, when you cut off your heart from me, you cut it off from everyone. You cannot freeze parts of you."

We cannot freeze our hearts in parts. Numb a section, and it affects the whole.

I AM SO MAD AT YOU. I feel like when our daughters say their newfound favorite word, "hate." "Hate you," they say to me sometimes when they are frustrated because they don't get what they want.

I feel like I hate you, God. I am so mad at you. I am mad at me. I am mad at everyone. Push away. I want to run away. I want to cut my wrists to feel the pain hiding inside. I want to let it out.

Weeks later, I tried to pursue Matt again physically. It resulted in freezing. Hiding. Curling up in a ball. No heavens opening up. Maybe my head was in the wrong space. Maybe it was my heart.

I was terrified to risk again. To risk and lose.

I took my pain to God again.

Is oneness worth it? Is oneness with Matt . . . opening myself up to receive physically, emotionally, spiritually to him . . . with this hope of producing fruit . . . but maybe not producing fruit . . . maybe it won't take . . . maybe it will die . . . is oneness worth the risk?

I don't know.

Is oneness with you worth it, God?

Oneness seems to be worth the risk—even if the fruit dies. Even if the only fruit I get from oneness with Matt or with God is a more resilient Laurie.

It is sometimes agony to pursue you. It is sometimes agony to pursue Matt.

I looked up at our front yard, realizing where all of this writing was leading.

Do I love God for God himself? Or for what he gives me? Do I love Matt for Matt himself? Or for what he gives me? Can we continue to walk out this metaphor that has both sweetness and pain—even if the fruit we bear is not the fruit I want right then? Even if the only fruit we produce is suffering that produces character?

Could I do this? Could we keep working on our metaphor until death does us part?

• • •

MATT

Laurie had me read the end of her journal about the agony of staying one with me. It hurt deeply to see it. I felt bitterness and the desire to isolate creep in.

Ugh. Here we are again. She doesn't desire me. She's always running from me.

But then I paused. I have learned to listen to my emotions when responding to disappointment because they often tell me what I am really worshiping.

I could say to myself, "Self, you need to be *desired*. It's a Core Need! Laurie is not desiring you. Demand that she desires you."

Ding ding! I have trained my spirit to sound an alarm any time this angry disappointment sets in and the desire to demand grips my chest. That's an indicator that my needs are no longer needs but have become idols.

I can invite her and other friends to help me to feel *desired,* but I cannot demand from people. After all, they can help remove barriers to the need and represent God as the One who meets that need, but they can't ever meet the need themselves. They are just representatives of the real deal. Little gardeners. Little Christs.

I am convinced that God allows our spouses, jobs, and friends to disappoint us on purpose when we start looking *to* them instead of *through* them.

He loves us too much to let us worship anything but him.

That is good fruit.

Oneness always produces fruit—just not always the fruit we want.

• • •

LAURIE

Matt and I went out to dinner. I was fighting toxic shame, lies, hiding, running, and wanting to jump in front of a car.

Why did I get triggered again? Why can't I just be done with this?

I was fighting the desire to go back to Old Laurie. But as much as I reached for her—the one who resented Matt, wanted to hide, wished she could run—I couldn't grab her. She was like a vapor of me. If I really concentrated on those old feelings, I could make her solid, but I didn't want to. What I had learned about God changed me. Counseling. Visual prayer. Lament. Shredding shame. Old Laurie was a vapor I didn't want to be.

But I still felt terrible.

"I feel like I went backwards," I said, staring at my turkey burger. "I hate this. I thought we would be good now."

Matt put a fry in his mouth, chewing slowly. "Did you really go backwards? Did *we*?" I appreciated he didn't see this as my issue to be fixed any more—that the trauma triggering wasn't mine to bear. It was ours. "Did we go backwards or is this just something we will have to deal with as we work on our metaphor?"

I grabbed one of his fries. "Huh."

An image of a staircase came to mind. I had talked about discipleship with a younger woman earlier that day, and she had shared how when she battles depression or anxiety, she feels like any upward growth she had seen in her life is diminished. She sees her life like a staircase. When she gets into an anxious or depressed storm, she feels like she went down a few stairs and sat down. "How do you get back to the top?" she asked. "How do you not stay stuck in the bottom?"

I thought for a minute and said, "Toxic shame makes us stay stagnant. It lies to us and says, 'You're stuck. You can't move. And now that you are at the bottom, you are worth less.' Don't listen to that shame. Tell it to get lost and say, 'I may be here now, but I'm loved here. I'm going to take the step up I can today.'"

Could I not follow my own advice? Could I not give myself grace?

My soul was thirsty and in pain from all of the kicking and pushing I had done to it. "Maybe it's not a matter of getting back to the top of the stairs," I said to Matt. I drank that in. *It's okay to not be okay today.*

"Maybe it's more like uprooting weeds. I have one weed called 'attractions toward women.' Another is called 'assault triggering'—it grew up where the boulder was removed. Others are 'value from people' and 'value from performance.'" I took a sip of my water. "I may never get rid of these weeds totally, but their dominance on my mountain can change."

Matt jumped in. "And it's okay if they aren't removed completely. These are our thorns in the flesh. Temptations. Painful places in our lives. These are just our weeds."

Yeah, these are just our weeds.

I felt a weight removed. Getting triggered again after all of this work wasn't a sign of my lack of healing. Wrestling with attractions toward whomever was not a sign I am not surrendered.

Being tempted to find my identity in my work or in people's perceptions of me is not an indicator of my weak faith. These are just our weeds—temptations, wounds, thorns in the flesh.

I sighed, my soul resting. I picked up my burger. "These are just our weeds."

• • •

MATT

It seems after a few years into marriage, couples discover, "Okay. These are our issues. We need to work on them." After busting through a layer of the tough ones—like sex, in-laws, or parenting—the couple is prepared to sigh in relief. "Done. Got it. Check it off the list." However, as soon as they say "Check!" they turn around and realize, "Wait, you again? Why aren't we actually done with these issues?" Frustration is followed by toxic shame, which can lead to hiding that can turn into a marriage of cordiality but not oneness. It's easier to just . . . not work on oneness.

But maybe it would help if we realized marital oneness isn't a checklist; it's a garden to be cultivated. Gardens are never done. Even after planning and planting all of your plots, there is mulching, watering, waiting, weeding, and constant upkeep. And at the end of the planting season comes the next year with new planning, planting, and weeding.

As the years roll on, we may hope to obliterate some weed types or eliminate them simply with a gentle pull, but some are just our weeds. They linger. We brought them in from our single days, and we still have them.

Laurie brought a few of her own varieties into our marriage: attraction toward women, trauma recovery, people pleasing, and a performance-based identity. I added attraction toward women, seeing myself as worthless, and avoidance of conflict.

Both of us would love to check these off of the list, to stand at the top of the winner's podium and receive our gold marriage medal. Some days are like that. We stand in our gardens, lush with fruit, high-fiving, feasting, and watching Holy Spirit water trickle down through our gardens, picking up nutrients that feed oneness. Other days we find ourselves outside of each garden, frustrated by the growing weeds, and we say to each other, "Here again?"

When we find ourselves at the start of another round of weeding the same issue, I tend to feel sad, defeated, and ready to walk away. Laurie tends to sit outside of each garden in toxic shame and self-hatred. She wants to avoid, too, but she buries herself instead of running away like me. We avoid but differently.

"We are here *again*?" we ask. "These stupid weeds are *still* a part of our mountain? Why does it have to be this way?"

I wish there were another way than God using suffering and trials to refine us, but we would do well to remember that God's desire for us in a post-fall world is not to remove all the weeds or problems from our lives but to develop character and spiritual strength as we cultivate our gardens.

And we must cultivate. We have to stop the hiding, the self-hatred, the shaming, the avoiding, the yelling, and the blaming of our spouse for dragging this type of weed into our marriage garden beds. Instead, we have to take a deep breath, look up, ask God for strength and wisdom, call our spouses out from wherever they are hiding, invite them to link arms with us, ask our friend-gardeners to look in and give us wisdom, and put on our gardening gloves.

As we do, we will begin to recognize which gardening shears are best for cutting up a particular root. We'll become familiar with the roots that require a shovel, the ones that fight back, and those that require outside help to cut back. As we cultivate, we get stronger and wiser, spend less time fighting over how or why, and enjoy eating the fruit.

Those small moments of feasting are a foretaste of future glory when we will eat the wedding feast of the Lamb with Jesus.

There will be no more weeds in the new heavens and new earth. No more tears. No more sighing. No more fighting. No more metaphors. No more impossible marriages. Only the Marriage. Only the Reality.

It is that hope that makes cultivating our impossible marriage worth it.

• • •

LAURIE

Ten months after the miscarriage, I was in the hospital. My water had broken at ten the night before, and it was now two in the afternoon the following day. I had been laboring for a long time—and without any painkillers.

I thought he would come quickly—yes, *he*. I couldn't believe God was entrusting me with a son. *Have I really healed that much from my anger toward men, God?* I felt beyond privileged for me—a woman who used to wrestle so deeply with anger toward men—to welcome a man into the world. I think God has more faith in us than we do.

But this little man was stuck, turned sideways. Babies have to be in a certain position to work in conjunction with labor pains to come out. My pain was intense, but it wasn't turning my stuck baby. Matt was doing his best to push on my back in a way that moved him, and Sarah was next to me on the floor showing me on her hands and knees what moves to try.

Sarah and Matt—the same pair present during the last birth that served as the catalyst to wrench hidden darkness from our marriage. "You two are so different this time around," Sarah had said just an hour before. "You and Matt are so much more connected." I smiled a fully present smile at Matt (at least, as present as I could while contractions racked my body). He squeezed my hand and smiled back.

But I was tired. Tired from the last sixteen hours of labor but also from what it took to get to that moment, the miracle of a birth. An impossible birth from an impossible marriage.

I waited for the next contraction to do its painful work of pushing our son in the right direction, but I began to weep— my forehead on the hospital floor, my arms stretched out in agony.

I wasn't crying about the physical pain. I was crying from a deep place in my soul.

"God, help me! This is *so hard.*" I grimaced, letting the next wave of pain pass through me. "Please, help this to move forward. I am stuck here." Stuck in pain was a familiar feeling. I'd been stuck for hours. Days. Years. Tears streamed down my face as I recalled the hours put into this day, the weeks of walking to try to begin labor, and the years prior when I never dreamed such a day would happen. Like a movie in rewind, I saw the agony. Numbness. Daggers thrown at Matt. Matt letting them lacerate him. Wrestling with leaving. Wrestling with wanting to jump out of the window. The desire to rip off my own skin. Going to therapy. Weeping on running trails. Begging God to kill me. And hope. Waves of hope.

We had worship music playing in the room, and it wove its way through the scenes. Worship. Oneness. Light cutting through the darkness. Hope giving birth to connection. To oneness. To life. To the literal fruit of two becoming one.

I wept.

Sarah was crying. "Light is coming," she said as a prophetic prayer. "I see it." *Let it be so, Lord* . . . I prayed.

I heard Matt's sobs too. He usually saved his tears for after the baby was born. "Matt?" I asked before the next wave of pain hit me. "Why are you crying?"

"I wish my mom was still here," he said, letting tears fall for her for the first time since her funeral. "She will never get to meet him here on earth."

My tears doubled as I pictured her sweet face. She, a mom of two sons who she loved the best she could, said to me many times, "There is nothing like the sweetness of a son." She was desperate for us with two daughters to experience what it's like to parent a boy.

"Let's do this next contraction for Patty, okay, Laurie?" Sarah said encouragingly.

"Okay!" I said, snot dripping down my face.

I let the contraction—the pain, the suffering—do its work. There is rarely good fruit without deep suffering.

Not my will but yours, I prayed through the pain. *Break my body open to release the fruit you want from me. I will take the suffering if it means something good will happen. Not my will. Not my wants. But yours.*

It could have been a prayer for my whole life.

After this hospital floor lament, in the midst of the greatest physical pain I have ever endured, I came to the end of myself.

And the beginning of new strength.

As I waited for the next wave of pain to rack my body, something else took over. I felt filled.

I didn't just feel love, joy, and peace; I felt I *was* love, joy, and peace. God's presence so permeated my every fiber that I thought I would burst with it.

My son started to turn. The pain became productive. Only God can transform suffering into fruit. Only God can make beauty from ashes. Only God can create diamonds in a crucible.

Only God can create life from what was almost the death of an impossible marriage.

Within a few hours, there was no more suffering. Only joy.

"He's here!" Sarah said to my war-torn face.

Tears streaked Matt's cheeks. "He's here!"

I smiled. The tears had stopped for me.

He's here.

Suffering had produced fruit. Suffering had produced joy.

It was worth it. I smiled at his tiny face and hands. I held him gently to me. *You are worth it.* I looked at Matt and smiled. *This was worth it.*

Our impossible-without-Christ marriage is worth it. It's worth the struggle. Worth the pain. Worth the toxic shame shredding. Worth the study. Worth the healing. Worth the weeding. Worth the fruit.

One day, when Jesus says to us, "You're here!" and we eat the wedding feast of the Lamb and the Marriage begins, we will all say and sing, "He is worth it because he is worthy."

Jesus is worth it. Jesus is worth fighting for your metaphor. Jesus is worth cultivating your version of an impossible marriage to mirror the marriage of Christ and his church.

ACKNOWLEDGMENTS

First of all, thank you to Jesus who brings life from death, beauty from ashes, hope from despair, and makes impossible things possible. This book is absolutely yours. Thank you to our dear children who partnered with us in the gospel through your patience as we wrote this book. Gwyn, Juliette, and Ellis—we love you so much. Thank you for sacrificing even when you didn't understand why you were. Thank you to the best agent ever, Austin Wilson, and to Ethan and everyone at InterVarsity Press for your relentless support and wisdom. Thank you to our incredible ministry team, supporters, podcast listeners, family, small group, and friends. You know who you are. Apart from a miracle, this impossible-made-possible-because-of-Jesus book, ministry, and marriage wouldn't exist without you.

STUDY GUIDE

All marriages are impossible, and they are intentionally allowed by God to be that way so that we serve as a living, breathing model of the impossible marriage between Christ and his church. The Marriage between divinity and humanity is only possible because of Jesus Christ. Marriages between one man and one woman are only possible because of Jesus Christ.

This section is intended for small groups of married couples to dive deeper into their respective impossible marriages. If you are not in a small group, couples and spouses can also work through these together or on their own. (If you are single and working through this section, most of these questions will not directly apply to you. Thank you for creatively approaching them to get the most of out of this book!)

After each set of questions, you will find an *Introspection Section*. If you are in a small group, we envision you taking time as a group to think about, journal on, or pray through this part alone, as a couple, or as a group if the section encourages it. Planning this time into each meeting will ensure you do it. Consider setting a timer during this section to ensure your group has enough space to respond to the prompt.

If the *Introspection Section* or some of the questions take too much time or feel too intense, don't worry. Just do what God prompts you to do. (We aren't offended.)

May these questions encourage you to live out the full gospel metaphor of your marriage even more.

PROLOGUE: IT IS IMPOSSIBLE

1. Have you ever felt like your marriage is impossible?
2. How often do you see your marriage as a metaphor of the marriage between Christ and the church? (Have

you ever thought about it as a metaphor? Sometimes? Rarely? Frequently?)

3. How does this metaphor affect how you view your spouse every day? (A lot? Not at all? A little bit?)

4. Have you ever heard of a mixed-orientation marriage? How is it different from yours? How does it seem similar?

5. The authors have received bad advice about their marriage from others. ("Just have more sex with him—that will make it better"; "Just pray"; "You should leave him and find a wife"; "You should leave her and find a better wife"; "Serve her by cleaning the kitchen, and you'll get sex in the bedroom"; "I'll pray for you.") What is some bad advice have you received? What made it unhelpful?

6. Do you ever view sex as currency in your marriage? (Your body for his heart? Her body for your heart?) How does that make you feel?

Introspection Section. Spend some time praying on your own, as a couple, and in your group that God would use this book and study in the way he wants—not only so that marriages can be strengthened but so that your version of the gospel metaphor would strengthen the church.

CHAPTER 1: WHAT DO YOU WANT?

1. What first attracted you to your spouse?

2. Has there ever been a season of intense pain in your marriage? What was it like?

3. What do you think of the idea that there are those who follow their natural instincts toward ungodly desires because they don't have God's Spirit in them (Jude 17-19)?

4. When in your life have you followed your natural instinct? How did it go for you?

5. Is sex a need? Why or why not?

6. Reflect on the "What do you want?" question Laurie took to the silent retreat: When you were first married, what did you want your marriage to look like? Specifically think about friendship with your spouse, sexual interaction, and general joy in your home.

7. What do you want it to look like now?

8. What does God want your marriage to look like?

Introspection Section. Take some time to prayerfully take this last question to God. After some time of listening, reading, and reflecting alone, if you feel comfortable, share with your spouse and group what God brought to mind as a renewed vision for your marriage.

CHAPTER 2: A HALF STEP

1. The authors describe getting rid of *what-ifs*. What are some *what-if* questions you have wrestled with?

2. Laurie felt her fantasies were justified because of her past assault and sexual orientation. When have you ever felt justified to sin in your marriage? Perhaps it wasn't with fantasy, specifically, but with withholding parts of your heart.

3. Describe a recent time when you covered fear or sadness with anger.

4. How has trust been broken in your marriage? What do you think of the idea of writing practical ways to earn trust back?

5. If you are married, do you practice times of critical touch points? Why or why not?

6. No matter our season of marriage, we can always do things to feed more into our relationships. What is a practical half step you could take toward your spouse this week? Perhaps choose one of the specific ways listed in the book or come up with at least one of your own.

Introspection Section. Take some time to ask your spouse, "What is one way I could move toward you this week?" After listening and then sharing your own, pray with a same-gendered peer for God to help you to do that. Have that person check in with you via text or at the next meeting to ensure you followed through.

CHAPTER 3: YESTERDAY

1. What were your initial fun connecting points as a couple? How can you integrate some of those moments to stir the old places of your hearts together?

2. Which below are your primary Core Needs? Which do you feel you need the strongest or the most often because they are easily depleted?

   Affirmed: Overwhelmingly approved of (Psalm 118:6; 2 Corinthians 1:21-22)

   Desired: Specially chosen—no pretense necessary (Isaiah 41:9; John 15:16)

   Included: Wanted in this group, team, or partnership; "I belong" (Isaiah 43:1; Ephesians 2:19)

   Loved: Unconditionally accepted (Jeremiah 31:3; Romans 8:39)

   Nurtured: Cared for; held (Isaiah 40:28; Matthew 23:37)

   Purposed: Filled with a sense of profoundly mattering (Psalm 57:2; Romans 8:28)

   Rested: Re-centered and reset in mind, body, and spirit; includes having fun (Exodus 23:12; Psalm 127:2)

   Delighted In: Seen as unique and special (Psalm 139:14; 1 Corinthians 12:27)

   Protected: Unafraid; trusting everything is under control (Proverbs 18:10; Matthew 10:28)

   Noticed: Seen inside and out (Genesis 16:13; Psalm 139:7-8, 11-12)

3. Where do you usually turn before looking to God to meet your primary Core Need(s)?

4. How can you begin to turn your heart to God first to meet these needs?

Introspection Section. In quiet reflection, prayerfully ask, "What need did I feel was met well growing up as a kid?" Then, "What wasn't met well or in a way I needed?" After writing down your responses, ask God to help you answer, "What need is met well in our marriage?" Then, "What isn't in a way I feel I need?" Lastly, "God? Am I looking to you to meet these needs? Where and how am I not?"

CHAPTER 4: THE PURPOSE

1. What do you think of this definition of the purpose of marriage? "The purpose of marriage is to serve as a visible representation to a broken world that God loves them and wants to be one with them."

2. On a scale of one to ten (ten being, "We are nailing it as best as we can"), how are you doing this week showing the world how much God loves them through your marriage?

3. How do you tend to view sex in your marriage? (The best? The worst? Generally okay?) Has it always been that way?

4. In which way are you stronger: physically or emotionally?

5. What would it look like for you to steward your strength better?

6. What would it look for you to step into your spouse's strength?

Introspection Section. Have a conversation with your spouse asking which area he or she thinks you are stronger in. Ask what he or she likes about your strengths in this area. Ask what intimidates (shuts down or aggravates) him/her about the way you step into that strength. Ask how you could better care for his/her heart in that space. (Note: If you are sharing how your spouse can better utilize his/her strength, use this type of sentence to be heard: "When you do [action], it makes me feel [emotion]. It would help me to feel safe in this space if you did [suggestion—not demand].")

CHAPTER 5: ONENESS, EVEN WHEN
WE MARRY THE WRONG PERSON

1. What is your favorite way to connect with your spouse (e.g., a walk, a date, having sex, playing a game, going on vacation, cooking together, in-tandem caring for the kids, a mission trip, etc.)?

Oneness Event: _____

2. How much does this oneness event cultivate each of the Gardens of Relating? (Think about it from your perspective only.) In other words, how high of a connection ranking does this event get on a scale of one to ten in your emotional, spiritual, physical, intellectual, social, familial, and stewardship oneness?

GARDENS OF RELATING	ONENESS SCORE: 1-10
Emotional	
Spiritual	
Physical	
Intellectual	
Social	
Family	
Stewardship	
Total	

3. Where do you feel the least connected? Choose three events (e.g., having sex, raising the kids, talking about finances, going to church, talking on a stage, at small group, on dates, getting home from work, etc.).

Oneness Event: _____

GARDENS OF RELATING	ONENESS SCORE: 1-10
Emotional	
Spiritual	
Physical	
Intellectual	
Social	
Family	
Stewardship	
Total	

Oneness Event: _____

GARDENS OF RELATING	ONENESS SCORE: 1-10
Emotional	
Spiritual	
Physical	
Intellectual	
Social	
Family	
Stewardship	
Total	

Oneness Event: _____

GARDENS OF RELATING	ONENESS SCORE: 1-10
Emotional	
Spiritual	
Physical	
Intellectual	
Social	
Family	
Stewardship	
Total	

4. Compare your answers with your spouse's. Which event is the lowest for the both of you? Which event has the greatest discrepancy (you rated it high, but your spouse rated it low)? Choose this event to focus on.

5. What surprised you about this event? What didn't surprise you?

   Oneness Event: _____

   Total Oneness Score for You: _____

   Total Oneness Score for Your Spouse: _____

6. Which Garden had the lowest rating for this event:

   For You: _____

   For Your Spouse: _____

7. Now, think about this event as it relates to Core Needs. Which of the Core Needs is being supported in this event?

CORE NEED	SCORE: 1-10
Affirmed	
Desired	
Included	
Loved	
Nurtured	
Purposed	
Rested	
Delighted In	
Protected	
Noticed	
Total	

8. Compare your highest and lowest scores with your spouse's.

   Highest for Me: _____

   Highest for My Spouse: _____

   Lowest for Me: _____

   Lowest for My Spouse: _____

9. What do you notice?

10. How might this difference contribute to tension in your marriage?

Introspection Section. Ask your spouse how you could help remove barriers for him/her during this tense event. After, share some ways your spouse could help you in the same event or another one. Then, ask the Lord to help you both to garden well alongside each other. You may want to do this aloud, in community, so that there is accountability to each other and your group.

CHAPTER 6: THE AWKWARD MIDDLE

1. How do you usually respond to pain? What is your default reaction to suffering?

2. How could you become more like Jesus in your response to pain?

3. Where are you today in your struggle with sin?

4. What Core Need do you think is driving your struggle? If that's too difficult for you to sense, what garden feels stressed?

5. Matt mentioned how he did not feel other couples had to work as hard on their marriages as he and Laurie did. Can you relate to that feeling? What makes you feel this way?

6. Where do you automatically turn when you feel empty needs inside (e.g., your phone, working harder, daydreaming about vacation, etc.)?

Introspection Section. Take some time with God to pray and think through, "How can I adjust this autopilot from feeling empty and seeking idols to being proactive in how I get my needs met?" (Examples: Ask someone to check in with you, set an alert on your phone to pause and pray, write something on your hand, or do check-ins with your spouse.)

CHAPTER 7: SO LONG, SHAME

1. What *really* comes to mind when you think about God? Is that the real God? Or a shadow of how you were hurt by those around you growing up?
2. What do you think about the difference between godly shame and toxic shame?
3. Where has toxic shame influenced your life? How does it feel to you?
4. When have you experienced godly shame? What does it feel like?
5. What pebbles have you crunched on, pretending they were real, nutritious, Holy Spirit water (e.g., a pan of brownies, exercise, work, porn, friendships, social media, etc.)?

Introspection Section. Think through a recent time when you either sinned or simply made a mistake. Try to find the three pieces at play in that moment: guilt, godly shame, and toxic shame. How did you respond to each piece? After reflecting, talk about the situation with your group and come up with a game plan for how to respond similarly if you did well or differently if your response was not ideal.

CHAPTER 8: WARRIORS

1. Why doesn't the church engage the practice of lament more often?
2. Matt said, "Instead of taking our pain to them, we swallow it. But gulping down pain doesn't delete it; it forces us to reach for emotional antacids such as overeating, undereating, exercise, drinking, sex, or overworking." What has been your emotional antacid for pain this week?
3. Do you visualize Jesus with you when you pray? If so, how do you see him? If not, why?
4. What aspects of practicing visual prayer feel comfortable? What feels uncomfortable?

Introspection Section. If you want to engage this lament practice as a group, here is a way you could do it: Take some time either now or before you meet next to write out some of your emotions regarding a situation. Describe the situation. Did you notice yourself recently responding to something greater or lesser than the situation called for? (Examples: Your kid spilled his milk, and you got very angry? Your husband was late from work, and you were beyond anxious? Something terrible happened to someone close to you, and you felt almost nothing?) It may be a sign there is something deeper that God wants to bring to the surface.

Write to God an unedited psalm of lament. (Unedited is key as most of us are not poets and editing won't get the raw emotions out.) Here's a basic form of how Matt and Laurie recommend doing it:

1. Start with the *what* of that situation and write about it. What happened?

2. How did you respond?

3. How did it make you feel?

4. What did you believe about yourself, the world, and God as a result?

5. If you don't feel like you're getting all that is inside out into your lament, imagine transparency paper covering the scene, and then take an imaginary crayon to it. The crayon will pick up the essence or the emotion of the scene. Hold onto that paper in your mind's eye as you fly backward in your life, as if scrolling fast through pictures on your phone. Then, stop when that essence or feeling etched onto that transparency paper matches a scene from your past. Continue writing there, but start from the top of this list of questions with this new scene.

6. Bring what you wrote to your group next week.

7. Together, start with prayer, and when you feel ready, read it to God.

8. Your group can spend some time quietly listening after you share and offer a prayer, a verse, a picture, or something for you. (Make sure anything that is said is filtered through the Bible.)

9. It may help to have someone write down what people pray or speak over you.

10. End the time of prayer at a minimum feeling noticed and perhaps really receiving something deep from Jesus through your friends.

CHAPTER 9: NOT ALONE

1. What relational interaction stood out to you in this chapter?

2. What about it tugged on your heart?

3. Who are the pillar people in your lives?

4. Where do you see areas of growth that need for people to come alongside your marriage? (Do you need more groups? Fewer? Is there pruning within friendships that needs to take place? Different friends? Different ways you respond with your friends?)

5. On Brené Brown's list of unhelpful responses to pain and shame from friends, which reaction tends to grate on you the most?

Introspection Section. Whether or not we are in the midst of our own suffering, we are called to come alongside others. Who is God calling you to come alongside right now (e.g., someone in your group, your spouse, a literal next-door neighbor, etc.)? Take some time to pray about who and how you can serve.

CHAPTER 10: A GOSPEL PICTURE

1. Have you thought about sex in the eternal way described in the chapter?

2. Why do you have sex with your spouse? What's the motivation?

3. How could eternity become even more of your focus—both in your sexual expression with your spouse and in non-sexual areas of your life?

4. In thinking about the woman at the well, what does it do to your soul to think that God's desire for you came first? "Even before he made the world, God loved us and chose us in Christ to be holy and without fault in his eyes" (Ephesians 1:4).

5. How has sex with your spouse taught you more about the gospel?

Introspection Section. Now, it's a bit strange that many couples are fine putting their bodies together but feel uncomfortable talking about it. So, let's talk about it. (This might feel awkward if you are discussing in a group setting. If possible, go off into different parts of the location where you are meeting to talk one-on-one with your spouse.)

Before talking, pray together something like, "God, help us to speak heart-to-heart in this very sensitive space." Then, ask your spouse how sex is for them: "What do you like about it? What is not your favorite? How can I love you better here? Of the times we have sex, when have you experienced a greater knowing of the gospel through it? What could we do differently so that there is more of a gospel awareness when we are together?" To close, pray again something like, "God, everything in our lives is about you—help us to honor you in this space too."

CHAPTER 11: NEW LIFE

1. What types of weeds did you bring into your marriage (e.g., perfectionism, performance, avoidance, anger, sexual brokenness, etc.)?

2. What types did your spouse bring?

3. What garden do yours primarily effect? What about your spouse?

4. When was a time you both worked well to uproot weeds from your marriage?

5. What is a variation you brought into the marriage that has been extra challenging to remove? Why do you think this is?

Introspection Section. What is one thing you will take away from this book? How will it impact the renewed vision God gave you from your answers in chapter one? As couples, pray into this vision for another couple in the group. Lord willing, keep checking in with each other to see how their impossible marriage looks more and more like the marriage between Christ and the church—which is only made possible because of Jesus.

NOTES

PROLOGUE: IT IS IMPOSSIBLE

[1]Christopher West, *Theology of the Body for Beginners* (West Chester, PA: Ascension Press, 2004), 92.

[2]Augustine, *Sermo Suppositus* 120.8, in *Patrologia Latina*, vol. 39, col. 1986, ed. Migne (Ann Arbor, MI: ProQuest).

[3]See also Genesis 2:24; Matthew 19:5; Mark 10:8; and Ephesians 5:31.

1 WHAT DO YOU WANT?

[1]"Quote by Charlotte Brontë," Goodreads, accessed February 2, 2019, www .goodreads.com/quotes/6575-the-soul-fortunately-has-an-interpreter —often-an-unconscious.

[2]People ask me (Laurie) if they will go to hell if they are in same-sex relationships. I never say a clear-cut answer because I am not God. Paul says about judgment, "My conscience is clear, but that doesn't prove I'm right. It is the Lord himself who will examine me and decide" (1 Corinthians 4:4). God is our judge. However, whenever I read 1 Corinthians 6:9-10 in light of pursuing ongoing, unrepentant sin of any variety (including same-sex activity), I am sobered. "Don't you realize that those who do wrong will not inherit the Kingdom of God? Don't fool yourselves. Those who indulge in sexual sin, or who worship idols, or commit adultery, or are male prostitutes, or practice homosexuality . . . none of these will inherit the Kingdom of God."

[3]Louann Brizendine, "Love, Sex and the Male Brain," CNN Opinion, March 25, 2010, www.cnn.com/2010/OPINION/03/23/brizendine.male.brain/index.html.

2 A HALF STEP

[1]Gary and Barb Rosberg, "9. Marriage Maintenance Check - Four Points Of Daily Connection," Bible.org, https://bible.org/seriespage/9-marriage -maintenance-check-four-points-daily-connection.

3 YESTERDAY

[1]For more on brain scan studies of what happens when we recall trauma, see Dan B. Allender, *Healing the Wounded Heart: The Heartache of Sexual Abuse and the Hope of Transformation* (Grand Rapids, MI: Baker Books, 2016),

58: "While participants recalled the traumatic event, their brain scans showed that the area of the brain that processes language, Broca's area, located in the left inferior frontal gyrus, suddenly deactivated or significantly decreased in activity. Literally, during trauma, language goes offline." See also Bessel van der Kolk's invaluable work, *The Body Keeps the Score: Brain, Mind, and Body in the Healing of Trauma* (New York: Penguin, 2014).

[2]I wrote and received one hundred responses to an unpublic, un-peer-reviewed survey that mostly serves as anecdotal support to our story. Survey: "Marriage Survey" via Survey Monkey. February 20, 2019, and "Mixed-Orientation Marriage Survey," January 20, 2019. However, for further support, you can explore Noam Shpancer, "Laws of Attraction: How Do We Select a Life Partner?," *Psychology Today*, December 2, 2014, www.psychologytoday.com/us/blog/insight-therapy/201412/laws-attraction-how-do-we-select-life-partner. His article explores how familiarity, physical attraction, personality, proximity, and similarity all play a role in attraction.

[3]John Calvin, *Institutes of the Christian Religion*, trans. Henry Beveridge (Grand Rapids, MI: Wm. B. Eerdmans Publishing Co., 1989), 97.

[4]St. Augustine, *The Confessions*, trans. Maria Boulding (New York: New City Press, 1997), 35.

[5]Henri Nouwen, *Turn My Mourning into Dancing* (Nashville: Thomas Nelson, 2001), 31.

[6]Elisabeth Elliot, *Suffering Is Never for Nothing* (Nashville: B&H Books, 2019), 9.

[7]Elliot, *Suffering Is Never for Nothing*, 9.

[8]Elliot, *Suffering Is Never for Nothing*, 30.

[9]David Kinnaman, "The Porn Phenomenon," Barna Group, February 5, 2016, www.barna.com/the-porn-phenomenon.

[10]Jay Stringer, *Unwanted: How Sexual Brokenness Reveals Our Way to Healing* (Colorado Springs: NavPress, 2018), 105. We cannot recommend his book more highly for people wrestling with unwanted sexual behaviors. It can help you diagnose your own "whys."

[11]Jay Stringer, "The 'Whys' Behind Pornography Addiction," *Hole in My Heart* podcast, episode 57, November 2, 2018, https://lauriekrieg.com/podcast/the-whys-behind-pornography-addiction.

[12]Stringer, *Unwanted*, 98.

[13]For more examples of what people call core needs or longings, you can explore Richard Ryan and Edward Deci, who proposed Self

Determination Theory (SDT), Enneagram coach Beth McCord and
pastor Jeff McCord who wrote *Becoming Us* (New York: Morgan James,
2020), Terry Wardle and his work with Healing Care Ministries, or Kathy
Koch's book on her version of core needs called *Five to Thrive* (Chicago:
Moody, 2005).

[14]Brian J. Walsh and J. Richard Middleton, *The Transforming Vision*
(Downers Grove, IL: InterVarsity Press, 1984), 53-56; Andy Crouch,
Culture Making: Recovering Our Creative Calling (Downers Grove, IL: Inter-
Varsity Press, 2008), 107-110; Tim Keller, *Every Good Endeavor: Connecting
Your Work to God's Work* (New York: Penguin Books, 2012), 42-52.

[15]For a full list of these Core Needs, please see the study guide for chapter three.

[16]David Zahl, *Seculosity: How Career, Parenting, Technology, Food, Politics, and
Romance Became Our New Religion and What to Do About It* (Minneapolis:
Fortress Press, 2019). See also Jeremiah 17:9.

4 THE PURPOSE

[1]AARP Foundation, *Loneliness and Social Connections: A National Survey of
Adults 45 and Older* (Washington, DC: AARP Foundation, 2018), 4. www
.aarp.org/research/topics/life/info-2018/loneliness-social-connections
.html.

[2]It has been estimated that 15-20 percent of marriages are "sexless" or
have had sex less than ten times in the last year. Tara Parker-Pope, "When
Sex Leaves the Marriage," *New York Times*, June 3, 2009, https://well.blogs
.nytimes.com/2009/06/03/when-sex-leaves-the-marriage.

[3]For a beautiful and gracious argument about why sex is reserved for marriage, please read my friend Preston Sprinkle's blog, "Does the Bible Really
Prohibit Sex Outside of Marriage?" www.prestonsprinkle.com/blog/2016
/9/14/does-the-bible-really-prohibit-sex-outside-of-marriage.

[4]In one study, 84 percent of women said they have sex with their husbands
so that they will do more around the house. See Sheri Stritof, "What
Marital Sex Statistics Can Reveal," Verywell Mind, March 24, 2020, www
.verywellmind.com/what-marital-sex-statistics-can-reveal-2300946.

[5]Francis and Lisa Chan, *You and Me Forever: Marriage in Light of Eternity*
(San Francisco: Claire Love Publishing, 2014), 27.

[6]Chan, *You and Me Forever*, 43.

[7]Tim Keller, "The Freedom of True Love," September 21, 2003, Redeemer
Presbyterian Church, https://gospelinlife.com/downloads/the-freedom
-of-true-love-5327.

[8]Dave Beelen, "Hungry for God," January 7, 2018, Madison Church, www
.madisonsquarechurch.org/sermondownloads/2018-01-21-AM_Square
-Campus_Hungry-For-God.mp3.

[9]Brené Brown, *The Gifts of Imperfection: Let Go of Who You Think You're
Supposed to Be and Embrace Who You Are* (Center City, MN: Hazelden
Publishing, 2010), 26.

5 ONENESS, EVEN WHEN WE MARRY
THE WRONG PERSON

[1]Stanley Hauerwas, "Sex and Politics: Bertrand Russell and 'Human Sexuality,'" *Christian Century*, April 19, 1978, 417-22.

[2]Timothy J. Keller, *The Meaning of Marriage: Facing the Complexities of
Commitment with the Wisdom of God* (New York: Penguin Books,
2013), 121.

[3]GLAAD, *Accelerating Acceptance 2017*, www.glaad.org/files/aa/2017_GLAAD
_Accelerating_Acceptance.pdf. See also David Finkelhor et al., "Sexual
Abuse in a National Survey of Adult Men and Women: Prevalence, Charac-
teristics and Risk Factors," *Child Abuse & Neglect* 14, no. 1 (1990), 19-28.

[4]Catey Hill, "This Common Behavior Is the No. 1 Predictor of Whether You'll
Get Divorced," MarketWatch, January 10, 2018, www.marketwatch.com
/story/this-common-behavior-is-the-no-1-predictor-of-whether-youll
-get-divorced-2018-01-10.

[5]Ángel Manuel Rodríguez, "Images of the Holy Spirit (Latter Rain)," Biblical Research Institute, www.adventistbiblicalresearch.org/materials
/holy-spirit/images-holy-spirit-latter-rain.

[6]Nothing we do is ever only physical as we are holistic beings. But the
point here is more the emphasis on the physical as opposed to seeking
holistic unity through all of our selves.

[7]C. S. Lewis, *The Complete C. S. Lewis Signature Classics* (New York: Harper
San Francisco, 2002), 298.

6 THE AWKWARD MIDDLE

[1]Isabel Pastor Guzman, "How the Body Keeps the Score: An Interview with
Dr. Bessel van der Kolk," *Brain World*, August 14, 2019, https://brainworld
magazine.com/how-the-body-keeps-the-score-an-interview-with
-dr-bessel-van-der-kolk.

[2]Guzman, "How the Body Keeps the Score."

[3]Dr. Bessel van der Kolk. Module 2. 9:39-10:30. Dr. Bessel A. van der Kolk's
Trauma Treatment Mastery Course.

[4]Christopher West, *Fill These Hearts: God, Sex, and the Universal Longing* (New York: Image, 2018), 32.

[5]In her book *Healing the Fragmented Selves of Trauma Survivors*, Janina Fisher describes the fragmentation that occurs with trauma in childhood and the retrieval of "lost children" that is critical for the healing process. Janina Fisher, *Healing the Fragmented Selves of Trauma Survivors: Overcoming Internal Self-Alienation* (New York: Routledge, 2016), 19-21.

[6]Nik Ripken, *The Insanity of God: A True Story of Faith Resurrected* (Nashville: B&H Publishing, 2013), 158. This entire section is a paraphrase of pages 153-158.

[7]1 Corinthians 6:18; Ephesians 5:3; Colossians 3:5.

[8]Milton Vincent, *A Gospel Primer for Christians: Learning to See the Glories of God's Love* (Bemidji, MN: Focus Publishing, 2008), 34.

7 SO LONG, SHAME

[1]I am not the first one to consider this idea of godly or good shame. See Tish Harrison Warren, "We're So Unashamed We Wrote a Book on It. Three of Them, Actually," Christianity Today, September 12, 2016, www.christianity today.com/ct/2016/september-web-only/were-so-unashamed-we-wrote -book-on-it-three-of-them-actuall.html. See also Joseph Burgo's book *Shame: Free Yourself, Find Joy, and Build True Self-Esteem.*

[2]For more uses of shame in the Bible, see the "Shame" entry on BibleStudyTools .com (www.biblestudytools.com/dictionaries/bakers-evangelical-dictionary /shame.html).

[3]Timothy J. Keller, "Eating with Jesus" Sermon. January 30, 2000. Gospel in Life. https://gospelinlife.com/downloads/eating-with-jesus-5123.

[4]A. W. Tozer, *The Knowledge of the Holy* (New York: HarperCollins, 1978), 1.

[5]Dan Allender, "Sexuality and Shame with Dr. Dan Allender," *Hole in My Heart* podcast, episode 83, May 17, 2019, https://lauriekrieg.com /podcast/sexuality-and-shame-with-dan-allender.

[6]William Struthers, "Brain Science and Porn" Forum at the Set Free Summit, Greensboro, SC, April 5, 2016, https://setfreesummit.org/tuesday/brain -science-and-porn-william-struthers-donald-hilton-and-ted-roberts.

[7]Thompson, *The Soul of Shame*, 35.

[8]Thompson, *The Soul of Shame*, 35.

[9]What we do is similar to Formational Prayer, as taught by Dr. Terry Wardle. For more information on the subject, visit his Formational Prayer Seminar page at www.healingcare.org/formational-prayer-seminar.

[10]R. A. Torrey *The Power of Prayer and the Prayer of Power* (Abbotsford, WI: Aneko Press, 2020), 62.

[11]For more on the gifts of confessing to one another, see Dietrich Bonhoeffer, *Life Together: The Classic Exploration of Christian in Community* (New York: HarperCollins, 1954), 110-22.

8 WARRIORS

[1]2 Kings 5:14; Mark 8:23, 25; Matthew 9:20-22.

[2]Pieces of the interplay between Matt and Laurie and their praying through this memory together was first a part of a blog post on her site, lauriekrieg .com. Laurie Krieg, "The Day I Became Wonder Woman," September 6, 2019, https://lauriekrieg.com/the-day-i-became-wonder-woman.

[3]Branson Parler, "Episode 26: Marriage: What Is It Good For? with Branson Parler," *Hole in My Heart* podcast, February 23, 2018, https://lauriekrieg .com/podcast/marriage-what-is-it-good-for.

[4]It is similar to guided imagery narrative therapy combined with grounding techniques therapists use to help clients who are processing trauma be able to start and end in a place of homeostasis.

[5]Timothy Keller, *Prayer: Experiencing Awe and Intimacy with God* (New York: Dutton, 2014), 62.

[6]Ken Camp, "Absence of Lament in Worship Leads to Spiritual Stagnation," Baptist Standard, February 13, 2019, www.baptiststandard.com/news /texas/absence-of-lament-in-worship-leads-to-spiritual-stagnation.

[7]Christopher G. Ellison et al., "Prayer, Attachment to God, and Symptoms of Anxiety-Related Disorders Among U.S. Adults," *Sociology of Religion* 75, no. 2 (Winter 2014): 208-33.

[8]See also Matthew 4:1-11; 8:28-34; 17:14-20; Mark 1:12-13, 21-28; 5:1-20; 9:14-29; Luke 4:1-13, 31-37; 8:26-39; 9:37-43.

[9]"Fact: What is a psalm of Lament," ESV Online, www.esv.org/resources /esv-global-study-bible/facts-psalms-6.

[10]Camp, "Absence of Lament."

9 NOT ALONE

[1]"Anne of Green Gables Quotes," Goodreads, accessed September 30, 2019, www.goodreads.com/work/quotes/3464264-anne-of-green-gables.

[2]Please, for the love, delete this idea from your brain about me and others like me. Just because we are attracted to the same sex doesn't mean we are attracted to all people of the same sex. Let us work on our lust with the Holy Spirit and those closest to us.

[3]Paraphrase of *The Gifts of Imperfection* by Brene Brown (Center City, MN: Hazelden Publishing, 2010). Parts in quotations are direct quotes from page 10. The remainder of the list is a paraphrase.

10 A GOSPEL PICTURE

[1]Sheri Stritof, "What Marital Sex Statistics Can Reveal," Verywell Mind, March 24, 2020, www.verywellmind.com/what-marital-sex-statistics -can-reveal-2300946.

[2]Wayne Jackson, "Jesus and the Samaritan Woman," Christian Courier, www.christiancourier.com/articles/282-jesus-and-the-samaritan -woman.

[3]John Lightfoot, *A Commentary on the New Testament from the Talmud and Hebraica,* vol. 3, *Luke–John* (Grand Rapids, MI: Baker, 1979), 275.

[4]If we haven't said it already, we need to address abuse: self-sacrifice is not the same as allowing another to hurt you. To study the difference in further detail, see Gary Thomas, "Enough Is Enough," GaryThomas.com, November 29, 2016, www.garythomas.com/enough-enough.

[5]Gary Thomas, *Sacred Marriage: What If God Designed Marriage to Make Us Holy More Than to Make Us Happy?* (Grand Rapids, MI: Zondervan, 2008), 208.